THE HOLOCAUSTS
WE ALL DENY

THE HOLOCAUSTS WE ALL DENY

COLLECTIVE TRAUMA IN THE WORLD TODAY

THEO HORESH

Author of *Convergence: The Globalization of Mind* and
The Inner Climate: Global Warming from the Inside Out

Bäuu Press
Golden, Colorado
www.bauuinstitute.com

DEDICATED TO

The tortured and forgotten,
Imprisoned in the labyrinth of history,

The broken and bleeding,
Tangled in an impossible fate,

The burgeoning roar of voiceless sorrow,
Bursting the bandages of hate,

Endless waves of suffering,
Reaching and searching, and grasping for relief.

May we open our hearts and hear their cries,
And finally staunch their pain.

Special thanks to the Elephant Journal and Salon.
com use of the articles contained in this book.

ISBN 13: 978-1-936955-21-3
Cataloguing in Publication information
is available from the Library of Congress.

Bäuu Press
Golden, Colorado
www.bauuinstitute.com

CONTENTS

THE WORLD AT THE FASCIST MOMENT

Genocide is rare, or that is what we tend to believe. We think we can tally the number since the beginning of the twentieth century: if not four—the ones in Turkey, Germany, Cambodia, and Rwanda—then ten or twenty. The major accomplishment of this book is to show that genocide marks our world today and that mass murder is plentiful, whether we deny it or not. The history of genocides is at once a history of their denial, a dynamic process which has kept them relevant to us and which has prevented time from rendering them obsolete. The Palestinian *nakba*, for instance, did not happen seventy years ago; it continues to take place into the present and beyond. The Armenian genocide is current today for the descendants of those massacred a century ago because it has not been recognized. Only the Holocaust has gained constant recognition in Germany.

If despite that it does not become irrelevant, that is because it has undergone a functional transformation, having become a foundation for what Zygmunt Bauman called "hereditary victimhood," which in turn is the basis of a state that ties its legitimacy and security to the illegitimacy and insecurity of Palestinians, by subjecting them to a cold, long-term genocide. In a similar vein, should the rehabilitation of the Assad dynasty's regime in Syria continue, the slaughter ongoing for the last seven years will remain a constant companion to the six million Syrians forced to flee their country, with even more displaced internally, and to all the rest, including those Syrians who are pro-regime.

Horesh writes, "Cultures inordinately shaped by collective trauma tend to live in the past." In any case, the Assadist protectorate, which has preserved its rule by placing itself under the protection of Russia, Iran, and their acolytes, has a genocidal slogan: *al-Asad aw la ahad!* (It's Assad or no one!). The regime is happiest in other words when it imagines itself remaining in power *ila al-abad* (forever), as another Assad slogan says more frankly. This is a call for a permanent war against the future, and the slaughter of those who aspire to change. This form of "the politics of the eternity," an expression I borrow from Timothy Snyder, gets support from Eternal Russia and its leader Vladimir Putin, radical in his animosity towards democratic change. It has been naturalized by China, which amended its constitution so that Xi Jinping may remain in power for life. And it makes for a world suitable for violent nihilistic groups in our region, where nihilism takes an Islamic face (maybe in protest to Allah's defeat) and who aspire to impose their own particular version of the eternal, of a never-ending end of time.

I do not talk about Syria because I happen to come from this country afflicted with one of the most brutal ruling juntas in the world today, nor because Syria is under multiple occupations while Syrians themselves are scattered around the world. Rather, I speak of Syria because the Syrian genocide is met by a state of global denial, where the left, the right, and the mainstream all compete with one another to avert their eyes and formulate cultural discourses, genocidal themselves, to help them see and feel nothing.

In this "fascist moment," to use Theo's expression, the global order is showing increasing signs of failure. Meanwhile, the oligarchy that has appointed itself guardian over international law and security is the source of the most brutal actions in the world, particularly those of Putin's Russia, which is behaving like an out-of-control gangster in Georgia, Ukraine, and Syria, while the other global powers see cause for little more than a sterile show of irritation. It is reminiscent of Europe's retreat in the face of Hitler eighty years ago, and might even be worse, given that America today has its own Putin, who is also admired by the rising right-wing tide in Europe, as well as large portions of the left.

Perhaps we are living on the threshold of a major collapse like the Second World War, and can do nothing but be astonished by the shortsightedness and the drop in moral and political standards of the ruling elites of Western liberal democracies, stuck in struggles and wars of the past, helplessly unable to change themselves in a changing world: foreigners are suspicious, refugees are greedy, poor people are dangerous, Arabs are unreliable, Muslims are the enemy, Africans are lazy, and so on. All of them must stay under surveillance and cannot enjoy freedom. The fundamental danger, however, comes from somewhere else: the powerful and their clients. Democracy is in crisis because of the attack of post-industrial capitalism, in its neoliberal version, on the social functions of the state, and the rise of identity politics associated with it. The media, along with postmodern and post-truth ideologues, volunteer their services in spreading awareness of differences in identity and culture over every social echelon, with the goal of distracting people from social inequality. This mix of neoliberalism and identity politics, based on discriminating between people and covering up inequality behind cultural differences, is what lay behind the outbreak of the Syrian revolution in the spring of 2011. It is something you will never discover from the Western media, nor lethargic and clueless leftists, themselves opposed to democracy, who prefer remembrance over knowing present-day reality, as befits all *salafis*, even if these ones have ceased their *jihad* against imperialism, to which they insist on subordinating our struggle.

With every passing day, democracy loses its criterion as a project compatible with spreading social justice globally, the way the peoples of Europe and the West achieved their rights, freedoms, and a minimum level of social protection. Today, this West, which does not know how to be humble, is not only causing harm to others but also to itself, because it cannot get out of the hierarchy of nations, cultures, "civilizations," and religions, set up by none other than itself. This hierarchy is rigid and firmly entrenched and has no name other than racism.

Refugees and immigrants find themselves at the intersection

of identity politics, the erosion of the state's social functions, and the lack of a global vision or project. The crisis of democracy and social justice embodied by this expanding internal Third World, inside many Western countries, finds its genocidal complement in the internal First World of Syria and other similar countries. It is represented by the fascist in a necktie: Bashar al-Assad, with the facade of his elegant wife, once called "a rose in a desert" by Vogue magazine, before the start of the revolution and the shame of the Assadist killing season caused her to have the report removed. The Syrian Lady Macbeth, imported from Britain for the then "young president," with her "Western cultural upbringing," prefers to have her clothes and shoes also imported from the most prestigious Western outlets, just like her husband's expensive cameras. This in a country where 37 percent of the inhabitants lived under the poverty line in 2007 and 80 percent today, where the Arab world's richest man, Rami Makhlouf, just "happens" to be Assad's maternal cousin.

One of the biggest transfers of property in Syria's modern history is now taking place, including that of its land for the benefit of foreigners and powerful locals, made possible by the biggest population transfer since its founding at the end of the First World War. This transformation has a well-known name in historiography: settler-colonialism, where an entire people is replaced, and ownership transferred to the colonizing powers, the incoming settlers, and the natives who win their favor. This too will not be found in the media. One might find talk of the "regime change" that imperialism wanted in Syria, which ascribes the aborted struggle of the Syrians to forces of global domination that wanted precisely not to change the regime, and especially not to touch its security infrastructure, to use the words of Hillary Clinton. One will not find anything about the "people change" that the protectorate may remain forever, under the eyes and ears of imperialism, and with its approval.

In his book, Theo takes us to Palestine, Iraq, and the genocide of the Yezidis at the hands of Da'esh, to Lebanon, Yemen, Burma, and Nigeria. He does not limit himself to looking at genocides of varying degree occurring here and there, but also alerts us to the dangers of the annihilation of life itself manifested in climate change, which has been denied by the current American administration, the country carrying the greatest responsibility for it. Alongside this denial, America is also currently showing streaks of racism unprecedented since the Civil Rights movement half a century ago. In his recent book, *Racism: An Environmental Threat?,* Ghassan Hage looks at the connection between racism in its predominant form, Islamophobia, and environmental issues, providing us with Mr. Trump as a fine example of this correlation.

Today's world contains within it severely traumatizing experiences on a broad scale. The unaddressed and unrecognized traumas not only draw people to the past, as Theo says. They also drive them to retreat deep inside themselves, to isolate themselves from others, or give themselves the right to savagely attack others, with the excuse that they themselves are victims of injustice. I know this from personal and collective experience, and cannot avoid thinking of the danger of how thinking about trauma can itself be traumatizing, or how social life and meeting others, that is association and society, become injurious and painful. What do we do when isolating ourselves in a faraway desert, or the top of a towering mountain, or a remote forest is increasingly impossible on a planet populated by over seven billion? And if non-isolation generates the severest pain, and politics, with the state—its tried-and-tested apparatus—an armed force of mass trauma, whose heads display a mix of brutality, avarice, and pettiness? We are on the verge of entering an age where thinking ("a dialogue with the self," according to Hannah Arendt) is of no help, nor is meeting and dialoguing with others in overcoming our traumas or even coping with them. Since we are then filled with rage and, it is only a matter of time before we explode, we are faced with the inescapable danger of an annihilation greater than any other: the killing of all human beings and perhaps the destruction of life itself, not at the hands of ideological extremists or out of bitter political conflicts this time, but rather because of pettiness, selfishness, and denial.

The time to resist the fascist moment is now, and this book is both an ethical document and a call to action. It clearly says the world is united and needs to be analyzed and dealt with as a single unit if we are to aspire towards a less cruel world. It also says that "methodological nationalism" is an intellectual, political, and moral danger, and that solidarity is no longer enough. It is becoming more and more a relationship of power that soothes the conscience of those doing the solidarity at a cheap cost when they themselves lack nothing. What we truly need is partnership, to meet and to engage in dialogue, to think and work together for the one world which we inhabit together.

— Yassin Al-Haj Saleh,
author of *The Impossible Revolution*
Translated by Suneela Mubayi

INTRODUCTION

It can sometimes seem as if people fear nothing so much as being murdered at the hands of another member of their own species. But most killings are more a kind of murder by neglect. The greenhouse gases each of us emits today will likely kill someone, somewhere tomorrow – and yet few of us allow this to get in the way of our comfortable drives and plane trips. The meat on our plates more often than not represents the brutalization of untold millions of sentient farm animals – yet it is the rare individual who once-and-for-all stops eating meat altogether.

There are all manner of holocausts, each with its own concomitant sense of denial, but this work focuses on the collective traumas of genocide and ethnic cleansing and their vast intergenerational repercussions as they are unraveling in the present. The Jewish Holocaust has become emblematic of both the evils humanity might commit and the astonishing capacity we possess for denial. Somehow, the world remained silent as perhaps the most dramatic and murderous event of its history unfolded. And somehow, ordinary people in perhaps the most developed nation in the world not only excused those killings but often engaged in them willingly and enthusiastically.[1]

But even as the vast bulk of humanity denied the Holocaust as it was happening, when it was over, Holocaust denial was somehow enshrined as a sin more egregious in some circles than murder itself. Somehow, it has become more inexcusable to deny a Holocaust that is receding into the distant ocean of memory than those that are washing up on our shores today. What is it about the imponderable violence of genocide that makes it so difficult to approach in the present?

THE GHOSTS OF GENOCIDE PRESENT

Over the course of the late twentieth century, the Jew became an archetype of the eternally oppressed and a symbol of survival. As information about the Holocaust slowly filtered into mainstream awareness, fighting Nazis in defense of Jews became the cause célèbre of seemingly every political neophyte and lazy justice warrior, and nothing quenched the thirst for justice like the Jews who fought back.

The phrase "never again" became emblematic of their struggle. And while it may not have originated with the Jewish religious extremist, Meir Kahane, he turned the phrase into a rallying cry for militant Jews everywhere. Whenever swastikas appeared on the sides of buses, someone somewhere would be sure to thunder "never again." Whenever some obscure professor suggested the number of people killed in the Holocaust had been exaggerated, the phrase would echo across the media, like some primordial call to justice.

Yet for many of us who grew up with the expression, "never again" was more a slogan for ending genocide per se. Never again would we allow a whole people to be destroyed without speaking out. Never again would we allow the great atrocities of the twentieth century to be visited upon yet another defenseless and vulnerable minority. Hence, when we found the phrase and the monumental sense of resistance it implied being used as a justification for attacks on Palestinians, we were stunned.

How was it the victims were transformed into perpetrators and the horrors we committed ourselves never again to allow became a justification for yet more oppression?

The confusion seemed to lay partly in the power of the phrase. Much like the preamble to the Declaration of Independence, which was later used as a template for countless anti-colonial struggles,[2] the phrase neatly and forcefully encapsulated a whole ethos that could be applied to collective trauma everywhere. It was the quint-essential call to resistance.

The transferability of the slogan mirrored the transference of the trauma. A powerful meme had been generated in response to the ultimate human tragedy and worked its way through the collective unconscious of humanity. Everyone seemed to be stealing themselves against another cataclysm like the Holocaust, but as the phrase was adopted by different groups in different places it came to assume different purposes. How was it such a wide array of groups generated a common response to commonly experienced horrors and yet used it for their own purposes?

Despite the power of the phrase and the forcefulness with which it was articulated, genocide continued to appear from Bangladesh to Cambodia, Rwanda to Bosnia, Darfur to Syria. And in several instances, like that of the Rwandan Hutus and Serbian Chetniks, the genocide they perpetrated was largely inspired by their own commitment to never again suffer the horrors of genocide. If genocide continued to flourish it was thus often not in spite of the commitment to witness its awesome destructive powers never again, but tragically and ironically, because the commitment itself was so prone to inspiring preventive genocide.

Sometimes the antidote is much the same as the poison itself.

And just as we failed to face up to what was happening in the Holocaust, people the world over continued to bury their heads in the sand. Every time another holocaust unfolded, the media seemed to arrive on the scene too late, the heroic cries of never again rising to a crescendo only with the closing scenes of the play. It was as if we could not wrap our minds around what was happening and mobilize for action until it was too late.

Genocide not only continued to flourish throughout the twentieth century but may actually be making a sort of come back in the twenty-first. Genocide is arguably being committed against dissident Sunnis in Syria and millions of starving civilians in Yemen. The Burmese military is committing it against its minority Rohingya and Isis against the Yezidis. Each of these instances of mass murder will be explored in later chapters, but what constitutes genocide and who is committing it in a multi-national conflict, like that in Syria or Yemen, is sometimes difficult to tell.

For the purposes of this work, genocide will refer to the effort to kill off vast portions of some population – whether it be racial, ethnic, religious or political – but will also refer to the broad-based use of tactics, whatever their intent, commonly deployed in genocides – such as the mass starvation of whole cities and countries that has a tendency to destroy those populations. While the use of the term is almost always qualified and contextualized in order to satisfy the rigorous criteria with which it tends to be applied in other works, the expression is also hinted at liberally. There is simply no other expression so powerful as genocide to denote the repeated perpetration of crimes against humanity committed against a targeted minority.

There is something elusive about genocide. Seldom do we find ourselves condemning a genocide in the present and seldom in a place we know well. Rather, genocide tends to happen in the distant past in exotic and inaccessible locales, like East Timor or Rwanda. This can make pious talk of never again appear less a commitment and more a salve to ease guilty consciences.

Genocides tend to happen under the jurisdiction of collapsed states, where the rule of law has broken down and civil war broken out across the land. Not only do such territories tend to be inaccessible and dangerous, they are also often bewilderingly complex. It is hard to sort out what is happening in a place like Syria or Yemen, where countless states are intervening and several rebellions are happening at once. Experts on the region tend to be scarce and reporters must risk their lives to enter. Hence, it is not easy to pin the blame on anyone in particular in a place like the Congo, where several million people died as a result of fighting among a dizzying array of militias at the turn of the century.

Most of us do not want to think about genocide. We simply do not know what to make of the effort of some group to wipe another out. We cannot imagine the horrors of hacked up and tortured bodies, and when forced to look we cannot sustain the gaze. We comfort ourselves by turning away, fall back on platitudes about it being too complex, take up the line of the oppressors, fault the activists for bringing it to our attention, or simply blame the victims. Anything to throw off the burden of responsibility.

All of these factors came into play when conflict broke out in Syria in the late spring of 2011. Journalists struggled to get to the action, and when they did it was often too complex to convey to the short attention spans of their audiences. Meanwhile, there were too few specialists to tell the media affirmatively what was happening, and with the experts faltering, false narratives proliferated. Leftwing activists took their cues from the Assad regime and Russia Today, generating an array of conspiracies in an effort to control the narrative and prevent another intervention like that of Iraq. This left the general public dumbfounded and policy-makers charged with carrying out the will of the people paralyzed.

Somehow, it was the anti-imperial peace activists who were aiding and abetting genocide this time around. And as if in the grip of some myth of the eternal return or unbreakable genetic code, we yet again seemed hypnotized by the violence and lulled into paralysis.

THE COLLECTIVE LIFE OF TRAUMA

Moral commitments tend to fall apart in the face of genocide. This is at least partly due to the fact that most everyone with even a remote experience of genocide tends in some way to be traumatized by it, and the trauma breeds dysfunction and confusion, which makes sustaining moral action all but impossible.

Trauma can be a bit like a crime that has been so well hidden that victim and perpetrator alike forget what happened altogether. The clues that some monstrosity occurred might show up everywhere from fleeting pains and chronic anxiety to nightmares and phobias. And yet, the memory of it has been forgotten. Judith Herman notes in her classic book on its history and treatment, *Trauma and Recovery*, that traumatic symptoms tend to transmutate from culture-to-culture and one generation to the next. They may make their appearance through physical ailments in one generation and mental illnesses the next, psychic numbing in one culture or acting out in another. As soon as one generation of researchers have elaborated its symptoms, they will often assume a new guise, like a criminal hiding from the law. Meanwhile, there is a rhythmic cycle to its study, with research growing in fits and starts. As soon as the prevalence of the crime, say, child sexual abuse, begins to be uncovered, all of a sudden no one wants to hear about it anymore.[3] In this sense, trauma itself it much like the ultimate crime of genocide in that people will go to great lengths to sweep it under the rug. And yet, collective traumas like genocide itself are harder to ignore.

Collective traumas are a lot like personal traumas, only they happen to larger groups of people, but since their reach is wider they tend to have systemic effects, which over time take on a life of their own. Wars and famines, ethnic cleansings and genocides, mass terror attacks and natural disasters, are like psychological tsunamis, deluging a people with traumatic symptoms. And those symptoms tend to ripple unsuspected through their institutions and cultural norms.

People in the grip of a collective trauma tend to become paralyzed with fear and animated with anxiety. They either fixate on the memory of the event or else blank it out altogether.[4] No human is capable of fully processing the overwhelming panoply of sensations flooding their awareness in any given moment, but traumatized individuals are peculiarly prone to shutting out vast swathes of experience, and this ultimately distorts their sense of reality.[5] Whether or not the traumatic event itself is even acknowledged, attention tends to become frozen on it, as all other experiences organize around it.

The instant the plane strikes the tower thus becomes a transformational historical moment, memorialized for all time. The several months during which a people were shipped from their cities and forced to leave their villages – as in the Palestinian Nakba in which over 650,000 of them were ethnically cleansed from the new state of Israel[6] – thereby assumes outsized proportions in national memory. It will be contemplated in literature and poetry and made real through film. As time passes, narratives of the event will tend to become increasingly mythologized, rendering responses to it ever more irrational. Members of the culture thus find themselves in perpetual mobilization for fights long passed, boxing with shadows at the bottom of a dark ocean of memories.

There is something uniquely unconscious about collective trauma. It quietly entrenches itself in social habits and institutional norms. It makes itself felt in moral values and political priorities. And yet, even as it shows up seemingly everywhere, it tends to go unspoken, haunting the culture like a specter from another realm. When whole populations become transfixed in this way, it can cripple the culture. Whereas normal nations tend to focus their collective attention on future goals like education and development, cultures inordinately shaped by collective trauma tend to live in the past.

If you want to know how the archetypal victim became the quintessential perpetrator, you would do well to look to these dynamics.

It is not simply the victims of traumatic events who become caught in their grip. Perpetrators also exhibit many of the same symptoms. When soldiers returned home from Vietnam and the First World War, the traumas they carried back with them often destroyed not only themselves but their societies as well.[7] The soldiers were of course the victims of a system that had mobilized them for war; but they were also the perpetrators through which its crimes were committed, and it was often the war crimes they themselves committed that traumatized them the most.

Observers of traumatic events can also be traumatized, and not simply those who witness them up close. To watch the fall of the Twin Towers on your television or wait in anticipation of nuclear holocaust, as the Cuban Missile Crisis unfolds, is to become caught up in a vast collective trauma made all the worse for your inability to act. Observers of collective trauma are often left riddled with guilt and anxiety. They play the event over and over in their minds, fantasizing their heroic interventions and castigating themselves for not having done more.[8]

Consider the way Americans have dealt with the genocide of Native Peoples. There was no single genocide of Native Americans but rather hundreds of years of skirmishes on the frontier, punctuated by village massacres and the ethnic cleansing of tribes. Sometimes the federal government restrained the killings, sometimes they spurred them on, as in the Trail of Tears, whereby the Deep South was ethnically cleansed of Native Peoples, following the most controversial legislative battle between the Revolutionary and Civil Wars.[9] While local governments often put a price on the scalps of Native Peoples, it was only in California in the mid-nineteenth century where the state government became involved in a full-blown genocide.[10]

But the historical memory has been mythologized, with genocidal killings punctuated over the course of hundreds of years and countless jurisdictions being condensed into a single genocide narrative. The genocide is a thing that happened, which was carried out by the whole of the nation, whose conscience is now haunted and legitimacy drawn into question. Native Americans themselves have meanwhile come to be treated as sometimes sub-human sometimes super-human, but the real Native Peoples constituting a little over 1 percent of the population have virtually disappeared from view, a marginalized minority that cannot break the poverty-trap. The country is thus haunted by a genocide it does not understand of a people it cannot see. And yet, the guilt associated with looking back on the original sin is all-pervasive among liberals, while the brutality with which it was associated is core to the conservative identity.

Collective traumas are always political. They are political in the way they affect collective identities and their historical narratives – when a people suffers a major famine it will change the way they conceive of themselves and the world. They are political in the way they organize a people to meet collective threats in the future – when a people suffers a genocide it will change the way they mobilize for defense. And they are political in the way they require political responses – even tsunamis demand a response and the failure of governments to respond effectively can often spell their end.

Traumatic episodes are recorded in memory as the scripts through which future events are unconsciously assimilated. Thus, the roles assumed by victims and perpetrators in the Holocaust become the template through which Israelis interpret their relationship to Palestinians. The script assigns roles to victims and perpetrators, heroes and observers. And since most people are neither devils nor saints, roles are switched over time like those of the players in some great Shakespearian comedy. Thus, the victims of one generation become the perpetrators of the next, and the trauma itself is passed from group-to-group like some ineradicable cultural virus.

Greater awareness of this process may not provide the antidote to the transmission of collective trauma, but it can slow its spread.

THE PURPOSE OF THIS BOOK

Shortly after midnight of my first day in the Palestinian West Bank, I awoke to the sound of bomb blasts but a short block from the hostel where I was staying. The blasts occurred every minute or so for what seemed like hours and were interspersed with scattered machine-gun fire. As we stood before the wide glass, fifth-story windows, we could just make out the images of about a hundred stone-throwers and what appeared to be a fire growing in the building next door. The thought of a midnight evacuation amid heavy fighting struck me as unusually dangerous, but my overall sensation was less fear and more that of being mesmerized and energized. Then something inside me said to write, and at that moment academic researcher was transformed into activist-journalist.

This book began as a series of articles produced in the midst of research for yet another more systematic and objective treatise on collective trauma, but in the process of conducting research, passive observer was transformed into active participant in the service of peace and justice. Social media posts written from the heat of the action were worked into articles, which spurred more travel and additional articles, leading me through the Turkish borders of

Iraq and Syria, Lebanon and Greece, Bosnia and Serbia. It was these travels and the articles they inspired that became the basis of this work.

However, the bombing had affected me in other ways as well, and it slowly dawned on me that in spite of the fact that my body was unscathed and the results of the ruckus had been somewhat anti-climactic with only a single death, the experience had left me traumatized. And though the trauma itself was relatively minor and would be washed out over the course of the coming year, it was compounded by my own terrible decisions made under the influence of the anxiety it produced. It became easy to see how collective trauma might destroy a whole people, with each of its members making a lifetime of their own bad decisions, as the culture itself gradually disintegrated.

But it is quite possible it was my own ancestral memory of collective trauma that brought me to the West Bank in the first place. The term genocide was coined by Raphael Lemkin, a Polish Jew who lost 49 members of his family in the Holocaust.[11] Jewish names appear everywhere among the ranks of genocide scholars. And whereas many victims of genocide try to sweep it under the rug, it can sometimes seem as if Jews cannot get enough of it, using it both to excuse the excesses of the world's only Jewish state and as an inspiration to stop the next one from happening somewhere else, sometimes even at the hands of their own people. Perhaps this results from Jews being one of the most privileged groups ever to suffer a genocide, perhaps it has something to do with their high levels of education. Perhaps it comes from their early involvement in psychotherapeutic circles, where the comfortable disclosure of hidden traumas became so normalized.[12] And maybe it can be explained by their disproportionate involvement in social justice activism. While my own relationship to my half-Jewish heritage is slight indeed, all of these things seemed to lead me to Israel and Palestine like a moth to the flame.

Just as it is difficult to determine the exact relationship between collective trauma and cultural development, it is often difficult to tell how individual lives have been affected by the collective traumas suffered by their ancestors. Somehow, the members of a culture victimized by collective trauma appear prone to the same repetition compulsion first articulated by Sigmund Freud, whereby traumatized individuals seek out situations like those in which they were first traumatized.[13] Thus, Jews become genocide scholars and human rights activists, while the Jewish state simultaneously talks about ethnically cleansing and being ethnically cleansed by Palestinians.

If trauma itself tends to be elusive, collective trauma can sometimes appear simply cryptic. Collective trauma is a new field, which is largely in its infancy. And as was the case with so many other burgeoning disciplines, it is being approached from numerous academic disciplines simultaneously, and speculation is rife. It is for this reason that a work like this that is multidisciplinary and speculative might be most useful.

While the reader should come away with a greater understanding of collective trauma, this book does not pretend to be a systematic treatise on it. While the book often provides a structural analysis of highly traumatized cultures, its historical accounts remain rudimentary. While it has a lot to say about genocide, the experience of genocide is not the main focus. While it often takes the reader close to the action, it is not frontline reporting. While it is interwoven with philosophical and spiritual insights, it is neither a work of moral philosophy nor engaged spirituality. It provides neither a comprehensive overview of the Holocaust itself, nor those contemporary holocausts it asserts we all deny. And the book can at times appear a hodge-podge of related reflections. It is a collection of essays, after all, not a systematic work.

But the discerning reader should come away with a vastly greater understanding of some of the most important instances of collective violence and genocide today. They will gain through it a sense of the way collective traumas shape cultural identities and thereby reverberate across the generations. And they will almost certainly learn to face these traumas with greater equanimity and compassion. Toward this end, the book integrates historical inter-

pretation, political analysis, religious studies, cultural literacy, social psychology, moral reasoning, and practical philosophy. I can
think of no other work that brings so many perspectives to bear on
collective trauma. And yet, while it has been polished like a fine
stone through repeated revisions, it possesses about it an unfinished
quality that will remain open to revision. Thus, these essays are best
looked at as the opening salvos in a conversation.

Most writing tends to be more a process of thinking than we
tend to imagine. Each assertion raises new questions, each answer
reframes the subject, until the work itself evolves into something
entirely unexpected. It is for this reason it is often said that writing is
rewriting. It is an intellectual and stylistic process of re-examination
that might go on for eternity but for the diminishing returns of ever
more revisions. Thus, the philosopher, Robert Nozick, could say the
finished product of most books tends to constitute more a snapshot
of some constantly moving set of questions and answers than any
final towering achievement.[14]

It is easier to produce a book like this, where each chapter was
formed from the rudiments of pre-published articles, than it is to
flesh out a single concept over the course of a couple hundred pages.
For even as each article in this book tended to involve painstak-
ing research and explication, there was little danger the book would
veer off so far in a single direction that it was put in danger of collapse, like the Leaning Tower of Pisa. But there is also something
more honest and organic about its refractory design, where ideas
reverberate through the work as a whole, echoing across its pages as
they are continually held up to new lights.

The organization is topical with the topic of conversation always being some people subjected to a collective trauma and their
means of escaping its history. The book itself covers the genocide
now unfolding in Syria under the auspices of the Assad regime, Iran,
Russia, and Hezbollah. It probes the injustices being inflicted on
Palestinians by Israel and how they might be ended. It explores the
genocide being committed by Isis against the Yezidis and the way
their terrorism is impacting life in Turkey and Lebanon. And it cov-

ers the refugee crisis in Greece and the famines now unfolding in Yemen and Nigeria.

The essays of the first part explore genocide itself and are often more philosophical and speculative. The second part on the Syrians is probably the most morally and politically focused, exploring what went wrong in facing the Assad regime's crimes against humanity. The third part on the Israelis digs more deeply into collective trauma and the shaping effect it has had on their culture. The fourth part on the Palestinians explores the way collective trauma has impacted the development of their national identity while focusing attention on how to ameliorate the historical injustices they still suffer without generating yet more trauma. The fifth part on Isis ranges across the Middle East, exploring the refugee crisis and apocalyptic terrorism alike through the lens of collective trauma. And the final part, which is perhaps most true to the title of the book, explores genocide and mass violence in Yemen and Burma, Nigeria and the Congo through the lens of moral equality, asking why it is we are so prone to take their lives less seriously.

The chapters have been substantially updated since they were first published as articles so as to make them more relevant to the present. But several have been preserved in their original form so as to better capture the historical moment in which events originally unfolded. The timeliness of the chapters will be evident in a few of these cases. *This Is What Everyone Talking About Syria Should Know* provides an anatomy of the conflict in Syria and its many participants, making it an excellent background to the other chapters in the section, even though the passage of time has altered the nexus of forces on the ground. Similarly, *The Coming Genocide in Syria* was originally written about Aleppo, a year before rebels were driven from the city, and yet virtually the whole of it can be read to apply to the Idlib province, where the Assad regime is about to launch much the same type of assault at the time of publishing in April 2018. *The Decline and Fall of the Israeli Occupation* was written in what appeared an unusually propitious moment for Palestinians in the summer of 2015, but while it proved naive in its optimism, the proposals it presents still remain strikingly original. The preservation of its original enthusiasm is an act of humility and confession on my part.

However, it is just the opposite with *The Politics of Evil,* which turned out to present a prescient set of speculations about the nature and structure of Isis, when they remained something of a mystery to all but experts in the fall of 2014. Similarly, *Whatever Happened to the Yezidis* was written less than a year after Isis trapped 40,000 Yezidis on Mt. Sinjar in Iraq in 2014, before they were rescued by an American intervention, and yet it remains largely relevant today. *Genocide in the Summer of Hate* was written in that same summer of 2014, which seemed to mark the beginning of a new age of mass murder and collective violence. While less relevant today than some of the other pieces, it is an important testimony to everything that was being broken at that time. *Murderous Monks and Silent Sanghas* is similar in that it was written a couple of years before the full-on genocidal assault on Burma's Rohingya in the fall of 2017, and yet it captured the very structure through which it would later occur. *Obama Must Quit Yemen or Risk Genocide Under Trump* is preserved in its original form for the similar reason of demonstrating just how much can be told of a genocide from its earliest beginnings. But it is also persevered in order to tell a story about how our knowledge of events unfolded.

Thinking through the temporality of these essays reminds me of its irrelevance. For there is a timeless quality to collective trauma, which tends to linger in the background for generations, only to surface from beneath the cracks of a broken order when social tensions boil over. One can only hope that time will make these essays increasingly irrelevant, but all too often it is just the opposite. The collective traumas of today are all too often but the continuation of those from ages past.

The book can be read topically, starting with the sections you care about the most. It can be read an article at a time, starting with those that seem most intriguing. It can be treated as a guide book to contemporary genocide and collective trauma. And it can be used to deepen your compassion and empathy for the victims of mass suffering everywhere. I believe it is a book that can be useful to laymen and specialists alike, and it would benefit the world if everyone read it. I can only hope that if you find it to your liking you will write a public review and tell your friends about it.

A day may come when humanity cracks the code that will finally break the cycle of collective violence that makes us so prone to genocide. Until that day, we can quell the violence through understanding more about why it is happening and the people who are its ultimate victims, and working with greater wisdom to make it stop.

Theo Horesh
Oxford, United Kingdom

PART I

THE HOLOCAUSTS
WE ALL DENY

THE HOLOCAUSTS WE ALL DENY

In your lifetime, you will needlessly destroy relationships. You will take wrong turns and miss vital opportunities. You will find yourself addicted to the wrong people or substances. And at some point, in due time, you will make a complete and utter wreck of your life. There is a banality to our everyday tragedies. And as it goes for our own lives, so goes it for the nations of which we are a part. We will elect dangerous and deceitful leaders, support pointless wars, oppose the fight against genuine evils, join causes we later regret, and retreat from the world in ways we deem selfish. All of this is part of what it means to be human.

The philosopher, Hannah Arendt, described the way ordinary people, carrying out ordinary bureaucratic procedures, brought about the extraordinary nightmare of the Holocaust, calling it "the banality of evil."[15] But the scholar, Daniel Goldhagen, goes further in an epic study of genocide, noting that its evils are quite typically not only carried out, but actually driven, by ordinary people.[16] This is how in a country the size of South Carolina, Hutu militias could in but a few short months, in the spring of 1994, hack to death with machetes 800,000 fellow Rwandans. They rose early in the morning, gathered at football fields and worked in teams, hunting their countrymen and women, hacking and chopping their victims, and drinking beer and sleeping with their wives when the day was done. This too is part of the human experience.

The point is brought home to me when considering my own previous views on world hunger. Following a logic that was cutting edge for the early nineteenth century, but simply ignorant for the late twentieth, I used to believe that we should not do anything about famines, because famines are necessary to limit population growth – and if we do not limit it now, more people will die later.[17] The logic was faulty, because population tends to grow fastest in the most poverty stricken places, like Darfur and Somalia. And famines do not kill nearly so many people as clever environmentalists think, but rather prolong suffering through stunting and trauma. My logic was not only faulty, and my position not only inhumane. My failure to study the issue in greater depth was negligent and amounted to a sort of passive support for genocide. And the scariest thing is it is a common view among environmentalists.

Not only do we make a wreck of our own lives and nations, but in the age of globalization, we make a wreck of the world itself.

Something similar seems to be at work among opponents of genetic engineering, who whip themselves into a frenzy over its dangers, but seldom consider that the scientific consensus over the safety of genetically modified foods is comparable to that on climate change;[18] seldom consider its potential to bring greater yields to African crops like sweet potatoes and cassava;[19] seldom consider the rain forests that will be spared if we can achieve higher yields; seldom consider the potential to stave off hunger for hundreds of millions of people.[20]

The tragedy of this stance was brought home when Greenpeace convinced the government of Zambia to bar a shipment of genetically modified food aid in the midst of a famine. The president, whom they convinced, complained of Western governments trying to poison his people, so he let them starve instead. And Greenpeace chocked it up to a victory. Robert Paarlberg, an advocate of using genetic engineering to increase African crop yields, suggested however that it was a crime against humanity.[21] Perhaps you are opposed to genetically modified food for good reason, and perhaps you can convince me of the rightness of your stance. But it is quite possible, if the scientific consensus on its safety is correct, that your opposition would result in the malnourishment and death by disease of hundreds of millions of people, and for no good reason.

We can find something similar at work in the opposition to a no-fly zone in Syria. Peace activists opposed creating a safe-zone for the victims of Assad and Putin bombings, even though the bombings had killed hundreds of thousands of people, and the no-fly zone would have provided them a safe space from genocide. It is quite possible that opponents of the safe-zone were correct that it would degenerate into war, but it is also possible their opposition amounted in the end to aiding and abetting genocide.

Many readers will agree with these views, and many will find them frustrating and offensive, arguing the genocidal implications of my own views instead. But what is interesting is just how few of us ask how our own cherished views might contribute to mass-murder. And what is most astonishing is how few of us care. The Pulitzer Prize winning journalist Samantha Power, who served as America's Representative to the United Nations in the Obama administration, demonstrates in her exhaustive book on the subject that America ignored virtually every genocide of the twentieth century. As the death tolls mounted, a few brave voices cried murder and showed how we could stop it – but most turned away.[22] Most of us stand stunned, watching country after country descend into chaos; most of us do not ask why close to a billion people alive today are malnourished. Most of us do not even possess the language needed to argue it is wrong.

Both the Hebrew Talmud and the Muslim Qur'an suggest that "when you save a life you save the world." But there is a sense in which to waste but a moment is to destroy universes.

A friend of mine dedicated to accosting random people on the street and waking them up to the plight of the planet encourages people to consider taking some action for the earth that will add a single minute to the lifespan of the biosphere – a single moment added to the lives of trillions of beings. It is a beautiful exercise in empowerment and a testament to the powers of math. But it is also a meditation on the human capacities of creation and destruction. There is much we will destroy in our personal and planetary lives, but universes might also be born in a single moment. This too is part of what it means to be human.

THE ILLUSION OF COSMIC JUSTICE

Depressed and despondent, the haggard man on the border of Iraq told me of how he had just lost his wife and daughter in a crowd as they ran from Isis. He was a Yezidi, the smallest and most persecuted minority in the region, and it was likely Isis would turn his closest family into sex slaves. Whatever the outcome, neither his life nor theirs would ever be the same again.

It never ceases to amaze me how normal such stories feel when set in context. When everyone is suffering extreme injustices, extreme injustice can seem simply in the nature of things. The commonness of it all can have a lulling effect, inuring us to injustice through simple repetition. But the opposite is also the case: when few suffer such injustices, it can sometimes seem extreme injustices are just figments of the imagination. And this denial leads people to blame the victims and their advocates alike.

Voltaire vividly depicts these contrasting experiences of cosmic injustice in his magnum opus, *Candide*. The novella is named after a wealthy, young aristocrat, banished from a life of luxury for kissing the wrong beautiful, young woman. He had been taught that everything is for the best in the best of all possible worlds, but in his exile he is impressed into military service and almost tortured to death; he suffers the epic Lisbon earthquake and the Spanish inquisition, which hangs his mentor; finally, he escapes to the New World, en route to which the passengers relate their own sad tales of woe, culminating in an old woman who, among other things, lost a buttock to feed a party of starving men.[23] The story reminds me of the kind Syrian refugees often relate in conversation.

Everyone knows life is not fair, but nobody expects to lose a buttock to starving men. It can seem quite impossible that one fine day you would wake to the sound of voices in your head and upon examination discover yourself schizophrenic for life; or that over the course of a few years your country would descend into civil war, your friends and family would be killed and you would become a refugee. But the bottom drops out from beneath our worlds all the time, leaving us bruised and confused by the boulders we had so recently pushed uphill. Why is it when we feel secure the smashing of our dreams seems so impossible?

Psychological researchers have termed the belief that people get what they deserve the *just-world hypothesis*. It is a cognitive bias, variously present in much of the population, which leads people to ignore injustices. It leads to the blaming of the homeless and the dismissal of genocide – and upon reflection, it is patently absurd. The world is a flux of forces impinging on our lives, few of which have been brought about by our own actions. Hence, the idea that the world might ever be so well-ordered to give us what we deserve can seem upon reflection fantastical.

Yet even after having studied most of the major genocides of the last hundred years and reflected for decades on how people deny injustices to preserve their equanimity, it is a belief that persists in my own mind as well. Somehow, it seems impossible to me that you could live a good life, work hard, love harder, and in the end get hacked to death by a crowd of angry men. How can even someone who makes a vocation of confronting injustice half-consciously deny its existence?

The Buddha taught that all life is imbued with suffering and that we suffer due to craving. Not getting what we want is suffering, because our desires remain unfulfilled. But so is getting what we want, because nothing is permanent; sooner or later, all things change, and the things we hold dear will slip from our grasp like water in the ocean. Tragedy encroaches upon our lives at every turn. Each of us will die and many will die lonely and painful deaths. We will lose loved ones and suffer painful diseases. And few of us will have done anything to deserve such suffering. Like the Syrian and

Yezidi refugees, we are victims of a contingent existence over which we have little control. And if we were to view our misfortunes in fast motion, as if watching a movie on a screen, each of us would find ourselves caught up in a similar fate. How is it the belief in security still persists?

We shield ourselves from these obvious truths through the belief in a permanent self, which can freely determine its fate. Amid the shifting fluctuations of body and mind, perception and conscious-ness, we seek solace in the illusion of a fixed self. But the world is a charnel ground in which everything is constantly changing – and no one gets out alive.

The idea of cosmic justice seems to stem from a similar set of delusions to those attached to the self. The just-world hypothesis is the universal delusion of conservatism. It tells us that people get what they deserve and deserve what they get; hence, there is no need to concern ourselves with their suffering, for it is all part of a greater scheme of cosmic justice. To tamper with the order of things in this view is to tear yourself apart with the folly of needless worries and to risk the well-being of others through the convolutions of impos-sible schemes. Around the delusions of the just-world hypothesis we concoct complex metaphysics, religious edifices, and ideologi-cal arguments. But a cursory glance at the real world demonstrates their absurdity.

The experience of injustice is a special form of suffering, which tends to cause a special form of distress. Not only does the victim of injustice suffer their circumstances, they must suffer the thought that they did not deserve their fate. And often they must suffer through watching others enjoy what should have been their own just desserts. The pain is compounded by the suffering, which is deepened by the humiliation and magnified by the wrongness of it all. Numerous studies have demonstrated that such experiences of injustice lead to stress, causing increased levels of cortisol, disease, and early death.

Injustice causes suffering and it calls for a response. But in countless meditation centers and monasteries, over the course of decades, I have watched entry-level practitioners of meditation and spiritual teachers alike react to concerns over injustice with animated displays of denial. They deny the existence of injustices, argue against their importance, accuse justice advocates of projection, and castigate the concerned as reactive. Often they are right: reactions to injustice can be so strong as to generate their own neuroses, but just as often they preserve their equanimity at the expense of reality. Even Buddhist meditation teachers can fall for the just-world hypothesis.

The quest for security that it represents is present in all of us and creeps up in the strangest places. It is responsible for a good portion of the world's most tight-fisted conservatism. And in erecting an illusory wall before a contingent ocean of impermanence and suffering, it actually increases our insecurity, for the truck you do not see is the one most likely to hit you.

If there is a benefit to being a refugee, it may lie in freeing oneself from just this illusion. The refugee knows everything is impermanent and that suffering is natural and normal. And this may account for some of the resilience to which this book bears witness. But it would be better if we could overcome our illusions of cosmic justice and face not only the causes of our own suffering but of state failure, genocide, and ethnic cleansing as well. There are many ways to overcome suffering and halting injustice is a good place to start.

LIVING UNDER TYRANNY

It was the moment he first began to chant for freedom that a transformation occurred.

He was a soldier in Assad's army at the time, at home on leave. But it did not keep him from protesting the regime, and when he opened his mouth everything changed. We met in a café in Greece, where he told me of his experience participating in several other protests before eventually escaping the country. Yet, now secure in Europe, his eyes shone brightly.

Another Syrian-American, Ammar, spoke to me of the way people in Syria used to walk around in a sort of haze. Everybody knew what everybody else knew, but nobody could say it – and when they finally opened their mouths, it was revolutionary. Perhaps there is always something revolutionary in saying what has sat bitter and suppressed on the tongue for years, and the transformations that occur are typically overwhelming.

The Cameroonian philosopher, Ajume Wingo, writes movingly, in a yet unpublished manuscript, on freedom and what it means to live under tyranny. "Freedom... implies independence and action that is often out of step with what is expected or tolerated. To act in such a way can be frightening." And because it is frightening, people living under tyrannical regimes often retreat by either emigrating or hiding in the womb of their own minds. "We see people petrified into apelike imitators before tyrants and their threats to any independent action. We see the fear-struck faces of victims of genocides who find it easier to march docilely to what they know will be their deaths than to defy their persecutors." And perhaps, it is this sense of terror that people living in developed democracies cannot comprehend.

It is common to hear so-called peace activists speak about their "Syrian friends" who are grateful for the quietude they enjoyed under Assad's rule—or their Russian friends who admire their patriarch Putin, in spite of his devastation of democratic institutions. Russians may no longer possess the ability to safely speak out against empire or homophobia, nationalism or the rule of oligarchs, but it is argued they feel secure and that is what matters most. But this is a shallow notion of human flourishing, and it fails to seek out any meaning behind what the victims are saying.

Complain to the telephone support staff of a major corporation about its service, or the manager of a fast food restaurant about the quality of its ingredients, and you will probably hear a similar story. No one likes to have their lack of freedom pointed out, because there is shame in the acquiescence to authority. And in pointing it out you are holding up a mirror to their spiritual self-mutilation. Wingo explains that perhaps, "The most terrifying quality of an autocratic or totalitarian regime is not the regime's ability to stymie political participation...but the ease with which persons are transformed into bare humans, fit objects to serve as the canvas of the tyrant's vision of the world." And it is this lack of agency, this hollowness at the heart of personal action, that points out the tragedy of tyranny.

There is something hauntingly surreal about the way the more intelligent Syrian supporters of Assad defend his regime on social media. It is not simply the way they mouth propaganda, saying Syrians love Assad, in spite of their fleeing the country in droves; or that Assad is the only force of secularism, in spite of his own military being dwarfed in numbers by the Iranian Revolutionary Guard[24] and Hezbollah occupying a substantial portion of the territory typically cited as regime controlled.[25] Nor is it that these slogans are so divorced from reality. Rather, the words are so audacious in their denial of reality, so void of moral meaning, so poised to excuse the worst atrocities, that they lift off the page in flight and drift about in a sort of dream-space. Words like these are drugs that allow people to escape the pain of existence and float about in their own fantasies of freedom. And yet, the fantasy of freedom is an escape from true freedom.

This retreat from freedom also happens in the developed world, where people suffer not from too little, but too much freedom. The social-psychologist, Erich Fromm, points out in his now classic, *Escape from Freedom,* that the burden of freedom can be painful and that many will seek to throw it off. There is a kind of sadomasochistic symbiosis between tyrants and their followers. The follower feels weak and insecure and seeks a great leader from whom he can not only get guidance but in whom he can immerse his identity. And so he immerses himself in the greatness of the leader, who embodies his own fantasized freedom, without the burden of responsibility.[26]

Writing at the end of the Second World War, Fromm was addressing a fascism that was about to be struck a death blow, but it is newly re-emergent in the world today. We can see it in the movement to elect Trump, where weak followers lapped up the repeated lies of their leader, where they reveled in his self-inflation and ultimately surrendered their freedom to a tyrant. Trump the bigot, Trump the sexist, and Trump the know-nothing braggart was transfigured into the savior that might magically break the power of the elites. The neuroses invested in this fantasy were simply staggering.

Fromm writes of freedom as the ability to act spontaneously, but Wingo suggests something deeper, describing the free person as "the maker of surprises." The thoughts of free people are gestated in private and expressed freely in public, coalescing in unanticipated demonstrations, like the Arab Spring. When Egyptian protesters took Tahrir Square in the waning days of 2010, they were not only calling for democracy but for a new freedom of expression at whose heart lay a tolerance for difference that surprised almost everyone. But Egyptians retreated from those calls for freedom in first electing the more conservative Muslim Brotherhood and then taking to the streets in support of a coup.

About the only country where the demonstrations resulted in full-fledged democracy was the place where they began. A Tunisian friend and doctoral student, Narjes Ben Ammar, speaks of the transformations that resulted. "We used to be fearful puppets, who dared not complain about their dissatisfaction even privately. With the revolution the wall of fear collapsed all of a sudden. That which we dare not allow our minds to think has now been spoken out loud." Yet, Tunisia is still in flux and roiling with economic and social discontent.

Professor Wingo suggests, "A community of free persons requires not just effort on the part of individual citizens, but also time to reach a state of equilibrium." But in a global community of increasingly free peoples, it might be some time before we reach the great equilibrium of universal freedom. In the meantime, it is disorienting for people brought up under democratic governments, who have come to take their freedoms for granted, to be criticized by people brought up under tyrants for their acquiescence in the face of tyranny. If there is an equilibrium to be reached among free people living in self-governance, perhaps there is an equilibrium to be reached among the citizens of emergent democracies and the escapees from the freedom of a democracy in decline. It is now immigrants like Wingo who may best understand the preciousness of the freedoms Americans so casually throw away. And perhaps the interaction between the two groups will make for the greatest surprises of all.

GENOCIDE IS NOW GOING VIRAL

Perhaps the most ignored news story of 2014 was the reappearance of genocide. The Syrian siege starvation and bombardment of cities looks like genocide. The Isis videos of hundreds of terrified young Iraqis being carried in the backs of trucks, laid down like logs, and systematically shot in the head looks like genocide. The recent ethnic cleansing of Muslims from the Central African Republic, coupled with Hutu-style machete mob murders and occasional acts of cannibalism, similarly looks like genocide. And then, of course, there is Gaza.

The capacity to commit genocide might be best framed as a social disease that spreads from group-to-group and is passed from one generation to the next. The Germans who forced Herero natives into the desert of Namibia in 1904, and over the course of the next three years sought to exterminate them all in the first genocide of the twenty-first century, later passed their disease onto others in this sense.[27] It is quite likely some of the advisors they sent to Turkey, who oversaw their genocide of Armenians, had some role in the Herero genocide, but perhaps genocide was simply normalized. Somehow, the disease reappeared in the Nazis a generation later. Perhaps we can trace no exact line of descent from general-to-general, perhaps German officials actually acted as a restraining force in the Armenian Genocide, as some have suggested. Whatever the inner psychological and cultural dynamics of their participation in genocide may have been, genocide can grip the unconscious and transform the norms of a military establishment.

Genocide is passed from perpetrator to perpetrator, but it can also be passed to observers who fear for their own safety. Genocides tend to spread in times of war, when there is carnage all around and more deaths might slip through the radar. But it is also passed onto the victims of genocide themselves. And this is the double crime of genocide, like a rapist passing HIV to his victim. The Hutus were themselves the victim of a partial genocide by Tutsis in Burundi in 1973.[28] After suffering genocide at the hands of Hutus in 1994, the Tutsi victims carried out mass atrocities against the Hutus and other groups in the Congo in the late nineties.[29] Thus, what most of us know as the Rwandan Genocide may make more sense as *the Rwandan Cycle of Genocide.*

Genocides can kill indiscriminately, for it is difficult to channel the drive to mass murder. Rather, genocide tends to take in everything within its purview. So, when the Rwandan Tutsis followed Hutus into the Congo in the late nineties, destabilizing the region and drawing in nine other African states, we saw an anarchy much like the European, Thirty Years War. Because genocides are indiscriminate, they spread panic. They stimulate the imagination of observers. And they set in motion cycles of revenge killings that can become increasingly intense, difficult to control, and similarly indiscriminate.

The collective trauma from this killing is then burnished in the minds of victims. It becomes a template for how the world works. The roles of victim, perpetrator, and observer are transferred from one to another. Much like suffering child abuse, suffering a genocide seems to predispose a person or group to later inflict genocide. Victims-turned-perpetrators live under the constant threat of annihilation, seek to avenge those who killed their families and guard against others who might do the same, as the memory of past hurt becomes emblazoned into their sense of national identity. Thus, the Palestinians appear like Nazis to the Israelis, as Israelis play perpetrator in a transgenerational drama that seems to never end.

To equate a people living under this perpetual boot heal of terror with the perpetrators who passed the disease of genocidal tendencies onto them can be like calling a rape victim by the name of her rapist. Nothing could be more insulting than to call an Israeli a

Nazi, for they are not responsible for whatever disease the Nazis passed on to them. But it is a disease that spreads, and it must be diagnosed. For genocides not only damage the victims but also the perpetrators whose power imminently crumbles, like the Hutus who lost control after a mere three months of slaughtering victims by day and getting drunk and looting by night.

When Israel Defense Forces organized and stood guard over the systematic slaughter of at least a thousand Palestinians in the Sabra and Shatila refugee camps in 1982, the idea that Israel might be capable of genocide entered Israeli national consciousness. Almost immediately, its Prime Minister and Minister of Defense were ousted by a peace movement that swept the country.

But as we observe the crowds gathering on the border of Gaza cheering on each strike, the politicians speaking of killing Palestinian women so they bear no more snakes, the young men chanting that there are no more schools in Gaza because all of the children have been killed, and the largely defenseless Gazans fighting a nuclear armed state after suffering a near decade siege with nowhere to run, many have begun to assert that the disease of genocide has reappeared amongst Israelis.

While Hamas could not begin to carry out anything approaching a genocide against a fully developed state like Israel for generations, and while they would almost certainly fall from power before that time might arise, they have also often spoken the language of genocide in the past, most notably in their now abandoned charter – and this sets off alarms for Israelis. Meanwhile, Israelis see genocide breaking out all around them, and it has been easy for them to see in Isis and Assad some future face of Hamas.

So, while genocide almost always goes unwatched for months, even years, with but a few reporters pushing the story, Israel is finding itself increasingly scrutinized for its genocidal tendencies. If they are exercising restraint, we should ask what a lack of restraint would look like. If the whole world is now watching, we should ask what it might look like if the world turned away. And if Israel has caught the disease of genocide and it is waiting to spring into action like a dormant case of rabies, we should ask what it might look like when the disease surfaces. Genocides, however small, have a way of tearing apart the social fabric of every group they touch.

THIS GENOCIDE TOO SHALL PASS

Hamas started raining down bombs on Tel-Aviv just as my plane departed for Serbia. Israel was then beginning a campaign that a delegation from the European Commission would later label genocide. It all made my long scheduled departure feel a bit like a getaway. My last visit to Serbia occurred just before the outbreak of war in 1990. Walking the streets of Belgrade, no one would speak with me, however good their English. The absence of anyone to tell me which food was vegetarian meant three days of surviving on McDonald's French Fries and ice cream, before stumbling across two monks meditating in a park, who later took me with them to Greece.

There is a tension in the air just before war breaks out, and something of that tension was palpable in Israel in the few weeks before leaving. But whereas the war in the Middle East would come to consume my life, the Balkan wars fell off my radar. Watching from afar, war would morph into genocide, but it did not even occur to me until many years later how close it had come to touching my life. Why some wars touch us and others do not can often seem arbitrary.

At the time, the Serbs identified with the Israelis. They too had suffered a genocide in the Second World War and were determined to never let it happen again. The Serbs suffered not at the hands of the Nazis, though, but rather the Croatian Ustashas. The genocide got so intense at one point that it even brought out the moderate in Hitler, who tried to tamp down Ustasha violence in an effort to bring stability to the region.

The Serbs were luckier than the Jews in the Second World War in that they had mountains to which they might retreat and build a resistance movement. They also had a long history of fighting back.[30] And their largely communist movement would eventually go on to build the state of Yugoslavia. The state would carry out one of the most interesting experiments in worker-self-management ever to appear in the world before everything fell apart in the early nineties. History has a way of generating novelty in the midst of the same tragic repetitions, but sometimes the most interesting changes come with the cessation of violence.

Waiting in the airport lounge for the plane to Serbia, it was easy to imagine the trauma in the faces of my fellow passengers. Their parents and grandparents had suffered a genocide. And they and their parents had carried out a double ethnic cleansing of Bosnians and Kosovars in the nineties. The Serbs had besieged the Bosnian city of Sarajevo, a major European capital comprised mostly of Muslims, who were remnants of the Ottoman empire that had for centuries oppressed their forebears. The Serbs spent two years sniping at Bosnian civilians in a modern siege of Sarajevo similar to, but more deadly than, the Israeli siege of Gaza.

But Serbia has become more prosperous and stable since the wars were brought to a close in the late nineties. The genocide against the Bosnians and the later ethnic cleansing of Kosovars were both stopped by NATO bombardments. And the Serbian dictator, Slobodan Milosevic, was overthrown through a strategically brilliant movement for democracy in 1999. And the leaders of that movement now consult with protest leaders around the world in an effort to foster democracy. Serbia and Bosnia are both growing more prosperous, if often too slowly. They are democratic, if quite corrupt. And they are largely stable. So, while the men in the airport waiting for the flight to Serbia were burly, they were also stylish – Europe is taking over in the Balkans and it is refreshing to see. Peace came like a thief in the night to the Balkans and now we take its stability for granted, as attention turns to the next latest disaster.

Most of us tend to turn our attention away just when things are getting good. The former Chief Economist of the World Bank, Paul Collier, once spoke with a group of Ugandan economists, who complained that no one would invest in Uganda. It turned out the only thing people knew about their country was Idi Amin, the brutal leader whose reign ended in the seventies.[31] Genocidal states do change, just look at Germany and Japan. And ethnic cleansers are often removed from power in ways no one might foresee. But the fighting continues in our minds, sometimes more so in distant onlookers.

Great evils are difficult to sustain largely because they are so corrupting. The band of thieves will sooner or later fall out amongst themselves; the genocidal state will sooner or later turn on its own. This sort of moral decay can be seen today in Israeli society, where inequality and racism among Jews are on the rise. Since these sorts of forces can be so destabilizing, the harshest regimes are often the quickest to fall. The instability of brutal regimes opens up a space in which higher development might be fostered, though. As Israel becomes increasingly aggressive, it is into this wavering space of possibility where we might find hope—for both a better Israel and a more livable Palestine. The passing of genocidal regimes can look from a distance much like the falling away of youthful fancies. Life goes on in Bosnia and Serbia, Germany and Japan, Rwanda and Uganda, Cambodia and China. Former victims and perpetrators of genocide alike often do quite well. For the human capacity for transformation is remarkable. And the nature of empathy is such that impossible chasms are often bridged through everyday activities.

Just tonight, as my weekly philosophy circle was closing a discussion on vices, a woman mentioned she was Israeli, to which a Palestinian friend replied, "I'm Palestinian, let's fight." As we laughed off the absurdity of our contingent identities, it was possible to catch a glimpse of how it all might end. Perhaps this seems a touch too idealistic, but if peace in the Middle East seems out of reach, it is good to remember that the Hutus and Tutsis of Rwanda not only share a small and fast growing country but often live together on the same hillsides – victims and perpetrators sharing an uneasy peace. And the Germans have become a rare beacon of stability in a union of European countries they once marauded. We would all do well to occasionally step back and look at such successes.

NAKED SHADOWS ON THE
ROAD TO DEVELOPMENT

A stark naked woman casually walked by me on the sidewalk. She was about 50 years-old and smoking a cigarette. It was a relatively busy street with only a few other people out walking, but they just minded their own business, apparently unfazed. She was not attractive, but neither was she repellant – she was simply naked. And she did not appear to be recently mugged, homeless, crazed, high-on-drugs, or making a political statement.

However, this was not liberal San Francisco or Amsterdam, but rather Belgrade, Serbia. Residents of Belgrade are not known for their bohemian ways. Far from it, the ethnic make up of the population is extraordinarily homogeneous, and there seems to be no real counter-culture of which to speak. The Serbs are perhaps best known for ethnically cleansing those who are different from them, though much has changed in the last couple of decades. Serbia is actually the first moderately well-functioning, middle-income country I have travelled to where there seemed little real income-inequality. The equality is probably a holdover from the communist era, and it seems to have provided for a friendly and relaxed culture in which people are largely content. They are generally well-mannered, mostly gentle, and have a strange penchant for obeying crosswalk instructions.

But then there was the naked lady, who seemed to have fallen so far through the cracks as to reside in another realm altogether. There are many things one might say about such a non-event. We might muse over how quickly humans adapt to the otherwise bizarre or the way clothing can reveal just as much as it covers. The Serbians have a flare for style, but this was not sexy. And perhaps the whole episode would have been forgotten in minutes but for the stimulus it provided to a traveller's reflections.

Serbia was the largest state of the former Yugoslavia. It was a communist country, run by the strong armed Tito, who is still revered for having held together the multi-ethnic states of what many regarded to be an impossible country.[32] Yugoslavia's economy was comprised of worker-managed firms in which employees selected their managers and the profits went to the state. It was in some ways the closest the world ever got to a truly communist ideal, and it is astonishing how little attention it has received. But those days are now long gone, fading memories of an impossible world.

When Tito died the country broke apart, and the Serbs held onto the rump of Yugoslavia under Slobodan Milosevic. In the process, they carried out a genocide against the Bosnians and an ethnic cleansing against the Kosovars.[33] The country was bombed by NATO in 1999 to stop the ethnic cleansing of Kosovars, and later that year mass protests succeeded in throwing out Milosevic and establishing a democracy. It was a beautiful moment in history that was mostly missed and is almost entirely forgotten. Now the country is on a path to European Union membership – that is, if the European Union can halt its own destruction.

All of this makes Serbia well worth talking about. It is a model of economic equality. It is developing without losing its soul. Its former system of worker-managed firms is a cooperative ideal. And it clarified its borders, put an end to war, and has begun to play nice – but nice countries rarely make the news. And as the world occupies itself with the rise of rightwing nationalists, we would do well to look at how a highly militarized state with insecure borders might resolve its issues and open up from within.

It takes great repression to bring a country like Serbia of the nineties to heal. The repression makes everything reliable and trustworthy, hence safe and secure. It is a process the nations of Western Europe went through in the early modern era, and perhaps it is a process through which they will need to pass every several generations or so as their precarious orders rise and fall and rise again. But when you compliment their country, Serbs seem discontented, hinting at hidden problems lurking beneath the surface, as if the violence might re-emerge at any given moment. And they are hard drinkers, tearing off the mask of normalcy when they do, as if this is their only outlet. Perhaps the naked lady actually was crazed or drug-addicted. Whatever the explanation, she might as well have been invisible. It was as if she was stalking through the Serbian unconscious, unnoticed but ever-present.

There is a sense that theirs is a flat world, and if you fall off the edges you will plummet into an abyss. It is common to feel such things in countries recovering from collective trauma. The wounds of history are often fresh and yet unspoken, making it difficult to tell the difference between realty and imagination. The naked lady seemed to have fallen off the edge of the world to inhabit what for most Serbians was wholly unconscious. But perhaps this was all just my overworked imagination – philosophers and travel writers alike have a penchant for overestimating their own mental powers. But if my musings warrant consideration, Serbia will sooner or later have to welcome its naked shadow into the party. Development is not only an economic and political process, it is also social. It takes a stifling degree of discipline to provide the reliability that results in Serbian social concord.

There are benefits at each stage of personal and social development. But the stage at which social conventions are solidified can be hard. Much will need to be repressed that surfaces later—or at least this is the way development has thus far worked. Sooner or later the naked lady needs to be invited into the party, and somehow her truths will need to be included. Sometimes it is obvious who needs to be included and the fight that this inclusion entails. America is now working to expand upon gay rights; last generation it was the rights of women. But sometimes the inclusion involves each of us keeping our eyes and hearts open to the uncanny, to the pieces of ourselves and of our societies that have fallen through the cracks.

HOW SOCIAL MEDIA
TRANSFORMED WAR

Every war has its own aesthetic quality. Vietnam brought us grainy images of hot jungles, protesting hippies and conflict at home. Iraq seemed somehow cleaner, with its bright sun, desert sands, and highly equipped soldiers. Even in protesting Iraq, there was a sense that it was over there in the abstract, measured in numbers and not the real human lives that were being broken.

Then there was Gaza – white hot and bloody, emotional and intense, anxious and brutal, and always personal. If you were protesting the attack on Gaza in 2014, the deaths were no longer measured in numbers, but in names and faces. And there is a good chance that a friend of a friend knew people there being killed, a good chance that by the time of the final ceasefire you had even made Facebook friends with people living through the bombing.

It was all so close that it sometimes felt as if you could taste the plumes of obliterated concrete.

Perhaps every war is like this for those more closely involved, but Facebook and Twitter and YouTube gave more people this experience with Gaza, and the global nature of the Internet blurred the lines of battle. When activists called Gaza genocide, it was not rhetoric, but the numbers never seemed to add up. Ubiquitous cameras and recording devices meant the world could see for perhaps the first time in history the collective hatred that goes into war making. Israelis were caught cheering on the bombings, dancing to the death of children, laughing as buildings were destroyed, and prank phone calling residents of Gaza, telling them their houses were about to be blown up. Whatever it was, Gaza *looked* like a genocide.

Not only could we now see the war up close through social media, the same platforms allowed others to drag us into it. The battle lines of Gaza were all too often drawn on our Facebook news feeds. Meanwhile, the supporters of Israel fought dirty. Trolls paid by the government mass reported innocuous pro-Palestinian Facebook accounts to try to get them shut down, researched the lives of their opponents and tried to get them fired from their jobs. They called protesters anti-Semites, attacked them personally, even threatened disinheritance. It sometimes seemed there was a generational war in each Jewish family and it was all on public display.

Each war has its own pace. Some are lightning fast, some build slowly like machines, some just simmer for decades. Because violence is so mesmerizing, people on the outside are pulled into it. Whether they take place in mountains or jungles or cities will thus alter the mood with which they are experienced. The mediums through which they are reported will also change their emotional tenor. Marshall McLuhan spoke of hot and cool mediums.[34] Television is cool because viewers are passive, and it takes lots of activity to grab attention. But Facebook and blogs are hot, because the engagement tends to be active and participatory. In this sense, Gaza was a hot war, waged in dense urban settings, where the damage was up close and personal, and anyone who cared to could join the fight. And it was a global war, much in the same way the Iraq War was global. But the fact that it was fought in the Holy Land, with all of its Biblical allusions, made participants feel more than ever like they were part of a global village. But it was a village that was being bombed out and doused with napalm.

There is an hallucinogenic quality to severe trauma, for we can be sucked into it like a whirlpool into which we gaze transfixed. This sense of swimming in terror pervaded the discourse on Gaza and it seemed to draw more people in than other wars. There was little room for reflection, little space to contemplate the next steps. And everywhere it seemed the horrors of the Holocaust were being used and abused by both sides. The idea that the victim had become the perpetrator now finally broke into mainstream discourse.

The fact that Isis was sweeping through Iraq only added to the intensity, for Isis evoked images of outright evil. Something seemed to have cracked in humanities' collective consciousness. The terror of the twentieth century was vastly more destructive, but Isis seemed to somehow rival Hitler as the source of all evil. And this seemed to affect the norms with which war was being waged by Israel. Everything seemed, all of a sudden, to become more brutal.

And yet, from Gaza to Iraq to the Central African Republic, where many also claimed genocide, the numbers killed were unusually small for the level of brutality. There were eyes everywhere and not only did this affect the tone of the wars but the outcomes as well. Isis took the aesthetics of war to new levels. A friend of mine pointed out that whenever Isis made a video someone had to decide which footage to keep and which to reject, how to splice in the look of horror on a young man's face, and how to pace the harmony of destruction. All of it was, in turn, crafted to match their specific brand of evil.

But everyone seemed to lose editorial control of their brands that summer. The Israeli Defense Forces came to appear in the eyes of much of the world as the new Nazis. And while Hamas became more popular at home, they came to appear even more unreasonable to an international media aligned against them. Meanwhile, Isis overshot the mark. While their videos were meant to strike fear into their victims, they were so scary that it sometimes seemed the whole world was ready to band together to stop them. Or maybe it was just one mass act of nihilism that was a secret even to the people leading it,[35] and the members of Isis were just seeking a new way to blow themselves up, only this time like lemmings racing together over a cliff.

And so we find ourselves in a new era in which spectator and participant are merging in war. Image matters more and affects us more deeply than ever before. The battle lines have shifted to new media. And the questions that now haunt me involve how we are to pace ourselves in response to the violence, how we can slow it down, reverse its course, and make it vivid without traumatizing a public increasingly exposed to violent imagery. Perhaps you remained on the outside in the summer of hate that was 2014 and all of this will be news to you – you would be lucky. Social media might brutalize us all by taking us too close to the action, but this growing set of participatory tools are the closest thing we have found in some time to the social technologies we need to tear down the house of war.

AND THE GREAT WORLD
KEEPS SPINNING

It can sometimes seem that events over the course of the last few months will make future generations look back on this as the summer of hate. The Israeli attack on Gaza has been devastating. The Assad regime in Syria has been accused by one State Department official of carrying out a genocide of Holocaust proportions.[36] The protests in Ferguson Missouri have brought extreme racism into the open in a way Americans have not experienced in perhaps a generation. And then there is Isis, whose videos of mass murder leave us stunned and haunted by the prospect of human evil.

It is possible that few of these events are related. The human mind has a way of seeing causal relations where none exist. And we tend to seek out patterns as a way of finding order amid chaos Perhaps events this summer have been just bad enough for us to begin looking for some sign that the world is falling apart. Certainly, Isis militiamen seem prepared for an apocalypse. But then again, genocidal actions tend to be a reaction to the perceived threat of genocide. Isis grew in strength as the Assad regime stepped up its besiegement of Syrian cities. And the Israeli assault on Gaza has been justified as a response to the genocidal language of Hamas. Meanwhile, Americans look out and see a much more dangerous world, and this collective experience can set police on edge. Perhaps we are all being brutalized by the violence to which we have become witnesses, and this process of brutalization is fueling a vicious circle of violence.

But the world is far too vast to take in at a sweep. My recent book, *Convergence: The Globalization of Mind,* explores how there is simply too much to know, too much to see, too much to comprehend for us to ever make sense of it with the same fluency with which we might come to know the nations of our birth. Rather, it is something with which we become acquainted only in flashes.[37] And this makes it easy to jump from one abstraction to another—the destruction of the rain forests, the persistence of world hunger, and the intensification of climate change can thereby appear to us a sign that we can only look forward to a future of destruction.

But then there are the optimists who look at the world and see everywhere levels of education rising, the lot of women improving, the lifespan lengthening. Because of its size, comprehending the world as a whole requires that we track more than just a few major trends. But since few have the time or patience to do so, our understanding tends to fail us when making a judgment about where the world is heading.

But then there is the summer of hate. Perhaps it is a consequence of having focused on certain events. The Isis videos are quite stunning, as is footage from Gaza. Many of us began the summer never having seen an actual beheading only to end the summer well accustomed to the sight. My Facebook newsfeed became a phantasmagoric theatre of dissevered limbs and crushed skulls. And all of this can be quite mesmerizing and entrancing. Meanwhile, the great world keeps spinning. And however much our chests may tighten, each of us keeps on breathing. As summer passes into fall, as the advance of Isis is halted and Israel slows its assault on Gaza, we are left with the same bewildering set of global trends. Education levels and temperatures are both rising. The area of rainforest cover and tropical diseases are both declining. The rights of women and the wrongs of police power are both increasing. And everywhere, people are a strange admixture of cruelty and kindness, empathy and hate.

The point is not to collapse the complexity of the world into trivial relativities. Nor is it to draw some conclusion as to where it is all heading. Rather, my goal here is to get you to step back and ask questions, to catch your breath and re-evaluate the issues that truly matter, to bring proportion to the most magnetizing events so that you might bring greater attention to the things that matter most. It is time to collect ourselves – always time to do so – and take this opportunity to ask which issues matter the most and which actions will make the greatest impact. While we may never be able to take in the world at a sweep, we can always get a little closer to a comprehensive view and that wide angled lens can guide us to what matters.

PART II

WE WATCHED A GENOCIDE IN SILENCE

WE WATCHED A
GENOCIDE IN SILENCE

The world sat silent as Syria disintegrated. We were silent when the Assad regime began shooting protesters en masse. We were silent when the regime began to bomb its people with chemical weapons. We were silent when Isis left Iraq and took over a large portion of Syria.

And we even remained silent as refugees began to show up on the shores of Europe.

The silence was only broken when it appeared the terrors of Isis would find their way back to Europe. And when we finally spoke out, we were so lost that the things we said meant next to nothing.

But the silence I came to know best was that of a particular community one would have expected to speak out – and loudly. The movement to end the occupation of Palestine watched in silence as not only Syria but also the Palestinian neighborhood of Yarmouk on the outskirts of Damascus was obliterated and emptied of inhabitants. We remained for the most part silent as 18,000 Palestinians were starved by the Assad regime, for two years, in the once-thriving refugee camp of 160,000.[38]

As Palestinians living there were reduced to eating rats and grass, most of us said nothing.[39]

It was a curious oversight, given the fervent solidarity with besieged and embattled Gazans. Here was the same thing happening in another country, but worse, and Israel had only a distant role in the tragedy. Whereas many Gazans were hungry, the residents of Yarmouk were starving. Whereas the *culture* of Gaza was being systemically destroyed, it was the *people* of Yarmouk who were being slowly killed off.

It was not as if Yarmouk was unique. Roughly half a million people were being besieged across Syria, and it was the sieges that were largely responsible for a tremendous portion of the four million Syrian refugees from the country and the roughly eight million or so more internal refugees. The Assad regime starves whole cities and neighborhoods so that the civilians will leave and they can kill off the rebels, thereby holding power through crimes against humanity.[40] When a treasure trove of photos of the torture, starvation and murder of 11,000 victims of the Assad regime, many with their eyes gouged out, was leaked in January 2013, the silence was deafening.[41]

We did not stop to think that these were simply the victims from one prison in Damascus and that there were still other prisons, and the numbers were likely rising fast. We did not try to estimate how many protesters were tortured to death and whether the systematic murders were still happening. The movement seemed paralyzed, much as the rest of the world – that is, if we noticed anything at all.

The paralysis sprang from several sources. Prior to the Syrian Civil War, the Assad regime had been perceived by many as relatively good to Palestinians. The regime never made a serious effort to criticize Israel, and was even allied with Israel for a time in the Lebanese Civil War, but its leaders talked up their animosity to Israel and activists took them at their word. Hence, when some activists started to criticize Assad they were often met with the fierce resistance of a small minority of fellow activists. This made it difficult to develop a serious critique of the regime. Many western activists who joined the movement to end the occupation during the attack on Gaza in the summer of 2014 also seemed to lack the moral will to challenge fellow activists. There was a sense that we needed to maintain a sort of united front, but as in the case of most paralysis in the face of genocide, the imperatives all seemed fuzzy.

And many of us were path dependent. We had spent years studying Israeli abuses in the occupied territories, building for ourselves a base of knowledge, networks and organizations, and were simply unprepared to nimbly switch gears and turn the Titanic of the movement around to focus on the confusing woes of Yarmouk, a mere suburb of Damascus, which was itself part of a country few of us knew well. And then there was the fear of Isis taking over should the Assad regime go. We seemed to think it was either one or the other, when in fact the two had hardly touched one another.

There was little talk about using diplomatic pressure to break the siege, or to just let in aid. Since aid was usually not getting through to Yarmouk, more pressure could have proven highly effective. Nor did we tend to consider the possibility of a no-fly zone as an alternative to Western invasion. After all, the weapon of choice for the Assad regime is the barrel bomb, a rusty old oil drum filled with chlorine, shrapnel and nails. Barrel bombs are commonly dropped on heavily populated civilian areas. Hence, a no-fly zone could have saved tens, if not hundreds, of thousands of lives. And it was what most in the Syrian opposition were requesting. But few of us engaged the issue deeply enough to see the potential. And we could not take Syria on its own terms, instead continually confusing it with Iraq. Somehow we thought that doing anything meant advocating a U.S. invasion.

Meanwhile, unsubstantiated rumors that Israel created Isis roiled, like some psychological defense mechanism against moral ambiguity. Somehow the activists who tried to speak out were shut down by this strange conspiracy, which actually had its start with Assad,[42] who suggested the connection between Israel and the rebels when he finally spoke on the protests a month after they started.

To this American of half-Jewish descent, the misinformation and obfuscation, dissociation and paralysis all felt eerily familiar. American liberals are all-too-often cowed into believing we do not know enough, or else that what we know might not be accurate, to speak out against Israel. And besides, we have other important issues, like climate change, to focus on. Thus, the Palestinians are triaged out of sight and out of mind. This silence in the face of what many would now call genocide in Syria was similar and pervasive throughout the movement to end the occupation. However compassionate and courageous members of the movement to end the occupation may have been, all too many were missing something profoundly important.

But when reports began to appear of Isis attacking the Yarmouk camp, something seemed to snap. The residents of Yarmouk were now trapped between two genocidal armies, one of which controlled a state, the other an area the size of a state. Reports spoke of the minuscule Palestinian forces facing these two rival armies. If Gazans in the summer of 2014 often looked a lot like the Warsaw Ghetto Uprising, facing down a vastly stronger power with little weaponry of which to speak, Yarmouk appeared a more perfect redux. The Palestinians had become the new Jews.

Since that time, Isis has been pushed out and most of the residents of Yarmouk have emigrated, joining a flood of Syrians that rivals the great waves of Palestinians pushed from the new state of Israel in 1948. Like the Palestinians and the Ancient Jews long before them, we can expect the Syrians to become a major new diaspora, pushed from the Levant and scattered across the world. As for the Palestinians of Yarmouk, a once distinctive community has melted away into a wider movement of Syrians struggling to make for themselves new lives in new worlds.

Yarmouk is but one tragic tale of a community destroyed by the Assad regime, which has done the vast bulk of the killing in Syria. And the movement to end the occupation is but one community that looked askance as a people whom it should have protected perished.

We have all turned away from Syria in our own ways. It is time we look more closely.

WHAT EVERYONE TALKING
ABOUT SYRIA SHOULD KNOW

The war in Syria has produced a whole lot of destruction and perhaps even more refugees. It has produced global chaos and an array of new terrorist networks. It has produced rightwing nationalism and a new world order. But perhaps its most sophisticated product has been its conspiracy theories. The Assad regime and its allies in Russia have engaged in what future historians may look back on as the most successful propaganda effort of the new century. But there are a few things everyone talking about Syria should know, and they would do well to start with where the conflict began.

The war in Syria began when the Assad regime assassinated[43] about a thousand pro-democracy demonstrators over the course of three months in the spring of 2011.[44] The demonstrators were typically shot by snipers, positioned on rooftops; but they were also killed in prison, where they were tortured to death, after being picked up by regime forces. The killings prompted defectors from the national army, who did not want to fire on protesters, to form militias in defense of demonstrators and their communities. Since that time roughly half a million people have been killed, the vast bulk of them by the regime. Most of the killing has been done through barrel-bombs, indiscriminately dropped on civilians by the regime, which has the only air force. And the bombings have obliterated massive portions of three of Syria's four largest cities.

The Assad regime terrorizes the local population until they depart, then mops up the poorly armed rebels. According to the U.N., the regime is currently besieging and starving over half a million people in cities it seeks to control. And it has tortured to death well over 17,000 detainees, 11,000 of whose dead and mutilated bodies were photographed by the regime itself and then leaked, as documented by Amnesty International. But the regime has disappeared over 65,000 people since the beginning of the war, who are seldom heard from again, and there are numerous prisons to which Amnesty lacks access, so this number is likely vastly higher.[45] Supporters of the rebels say they will never surrender because they believe that if they do they will be slaughtered in prison and their communities ethnically cleansed.

Anyone concerned with the suffering of Syrians would do well to begin with this recognition of who started the killing, who is doing the vast bulk of it, and why so many Syrians have become refugees. But the Assad regime is not operating in a vacuum. There are four principal local forces fighting in Syria. The Assad regime, an authoritarian dictatorship in power since the early seventies; the rebels, an array of militias fighting for a democratic state; the Kurds, a disenfranchised minority fighting for their survival; and Isis, which contrary to popular opinion, has not been fighting the regime but rather the Kurds and rebels militias, which have long united in opposition to them.

The militias that were started to protect protesters from the Assad regime were formed locally and loosely coordinated as the Free Syria Army.[46] The Free Syria Army was initially secular, but the Assad regime claimed the Arab Spring protesters who had taken to the streets demanding democratic change were terrorists. A virtual consensus of neutral observers has treated the claim as absurd, but the composition of rebel groups has changed over time, and the traumas of war and the search for weapons and funding have led many to join jihadist groups.

There are many imperialisms at work in Syria: Russian, Iranian, Turkish, Saudi, American, Qatari and British. And each state is funding and supporting its own favored groups.[47] But the secular militias of the Free Syria Army, which America is supporting, are by most counts the worst supplied. An Italian journalist, Francesca

Borri, notes that the Free Syria Army soldiers she found in Aleppo were so poor they did not wear uniforms but could rather be identified by their flip-flops. And it is for just this reason that many drifted to the better funded jihadist groups.[48]

The most prominent and problematic of these is the Nusra Front, which was started in Syria, but affiliated with Al-Qaeda early in its development to garner support. The affiliation was a mixed blessing, which brought in massive funding from Saudi donors but also the ire of America. Unfortunately, Nusra was by many accounts the most effective fighting force in the revolution, though its numbers have been quite small. And for much of the conflict they mostly kept quiet and protected Syrian civilians from regime attacks.[49] Nusra has often protected civilians, but it has also imposed strict religious rule in many places, and their presence has complicated American and British support for the rebels.

The Assad regime deliberately sought to foster a narrative from the very beginning that suggested Assad was the only thing standing between the jihadists and their control of the state. However, most Syrians say there were no jihadists in Syria in 2011, and experts on Isis agree that the regime is not fighting them in any serious way and did many things to foster their rise. Most importantly, Assad released key jihadists from prison in 2012. He did not fight Isis on numerous occasions when he had the chance; and somewhat astoundingly, he used Isis as his regime's principle supplier of oil, which constituted one of its primary sources of funding.[50]

The most knowledgeable Syria watchers tell me the Obama administration tightly controlled rebel access to anti-aircraft weaponry. This may have been because the Israel lobby pressed for this restriction, probably to keep them from falling into the hands of Hezbollah. But a more sinister interpretation says the U.S. wanted to prolong the fighting. However, if we take the Obama administration at its word, if we follow its strategy of their negotiations, or if we take the American desire to keep oil flowing in a stable Middle East seriously, a more considered opinion suggests the Obama administration wanted Assad to step down under a controlled and responsible transition. While administration officials may have occasionally condemned the war crimes of Assad and Putin, while they may have supported a handful of safe militias, while high ranking officials may have occasionally declared they wanted Assad to step down, most people closely studying the issue believed they were actually doing quite little to bring down the regime.

But the Assad regime is not nearly so stable and strong as people tend to think. Iranian troops now outnumber those of the Assad regime, which have been substantially depleted. And Assad has granted control of much of the country to the Islamist group Hezbollah. For years now, the regime has paid self-directing militias, dubbed Shabiha or ghosts, to carry out the worst atrocities. And the regime has allied itself with an array of militias, many of which have begun to come into conflict with it. Hence, establishing "state control" after the conflict is over, will be extremely difficult without some sort of national consensus, which would be unusually difficult under a regime which has destroyed many of its own major cities.

There are, of course, many ways of framing what is happening in Syria. And there are a number of major leftist journalists, like Seymour Martin Hersch and Robert Fisk, who tell a different story and have come out strongly in favor of the regime. This counter-narrative tends to be heavy on conspiracies and views the U.S. as the principal player in Syria. But Syrians, like the Princeton trained academic, Karam Nachar, have told me they find this view to be racist in its failure to see any agency among the Syrians themselves – as if Syrians could not start their own revolution.

Nachar also notes that it ignores the shift from a uni-polar to multi-polar world in which there are many imperial powers. To me personally, these leftist conspiracies sound shallow in that they lack a systemic understanding of the conflict; reactive in that they are more focused on what they don't want to happen than on what is really happening; nationalistic in that they treat Syria as if it is all about American foreign policy as opposed to Syrians themselves; and morally stunted in their willingness to overlook massive crimes against humanity.

My own narrative cleaves close to a virtual consensus among academic specialists, humanitarian organizations, and Syrians and Iraqis themselves, whom I have interviewed in several trips to the region and online over the course of the past few years. But what Syrians say the most is they just want the conflict to end. If this virtual consensus of experts is right, this may not be as easy as it sounds. And those who suggest it is may be causing more harm than they could possibly imagine.

THE COMING
GENOCIDE IN SYRIA

Scrawled across the walls of Assad strongholds, the graffiti taunted both prophecy and threat. "Assad or we burn the country, Assad or we burn the country, Assad or we burn the country."

It was a reaction to the early protests, when the people forecasted the fall of the regime, before the regime threatened back the devastation of its people.[51] Sometimes we let go gracefully, welcoming the unknown; sometimes we hold on so fiercely the intensity of attachment blazes the world to ash. In the end, Syria may get both Assad and the country he has burnt to the ground. But everything might have turned out differently.

The above words were first written from close to the Syrian border, in the Turkish city of Antakya, in the region of Hatay, where a Russian jet was shot down the day after my arrival. Antakya is an ancient town of winding streets, whose past glory can be descried in the managed decay of ancient walls and archways. Muslims, Christians, Alawites, and Armenians all live there in seeming harmony, a model of what Syria might have been. At the time of my writing, another world still seemed faintly possible. Now all of that is gone.

The last remnants of democratic resistance are fast crumbling in another ancient city, this time in Syria, where the otherworldly Aleppo is being burnt to the ground. Russian cluster-bombs are targeting the hospitals and schools of this besieged and starving city, as a ghoulish band of conquerors press in from every side. The Islamic State, Hezbollah, the Kurds, Assad, and Iran each press forward to claim their fill. And somehow, dreamers-who-believe-themselves-realists think it the closing act of this passion play.

Never trust the future to those who blind themselves to the present.

If Assad remains, little Napoleons will fight over the spoils. Resistance will go underground, jihadists turn to terrorism, Sunni fighters stream in from the Gulf. And the regime will almost certainly liquidate the rebel-opposition. This crackdown will involve mass imprisonment, and the regime that has already tortured to death at least 11,000, and probably tens-of-thousands more, the regime the United Nations has just accused of practicing extermination of its mass-incarcerated, will likely step-up operations of its prison-mortuaries.

Assad will see this as necessary to maintain rule, and the world will likely turn away, imagining the war is over. World leaders may watch in horror, and follow through with sanctions. Yet, the sanctions will make rebuilding the country virtually impossible. The economy will remain fissiparous. The stresses will exacerbate symptoms of collective-trauma, fracturing society into ever-more tightly-knit, ethnic enclaves. The bulk of migrants will not go home, as many more continue to stream out. Europe will feel the strain, and the flames of fascism there will burn the brighter. This epic-tragedy is not some play that will close with the death of its democratic protagonists.

If Assad remains, tyranny will reign, not just in Syria but also in the international domain. The dictator Putin, has already committed genocide in Chechnya and dismembered Georgia and Ukraine. His opposition has been imprisoned and assassinated. Yet, victory will put wind in his sails, dampening the blow of sanctions. And as the world turns away from an impending genocide of Syrian rebels, reactionaries will assail us from the left and right with tales of his unrivaled glory.[52]

Never trust the panegyrics of the passive consumers of state propaganda.

If Assad remains, it will be a victory for international anarchy.

Democrats the world over will feel a cold-wind bite, human rights advocates will sense their power waning. Sunnis and Shias will fight over the remains of a Middle-East dismembered, and the jeering bluster of anti-Western tyrants will rise to a chorus. If Assad remains, after staggering on the ropes for so many years, following the invasion of Iraq, freedom itself may suffer a knock-out blow.

Watching the slow-motion collapse of a country is reminiscent of the impermanence of all things. Much like the individuals of which they are comprised, states are fragile and can easily be shattered beyond repair. Antakya was a once great city of ancient Rome, but it lay at the hinge-point of several natural empires, the Persians, Greeks, Romans, and Ottomans; and the ravages of war eventually aged it into a forgotten backwater.

Something like the opposite is now taking place next-door in Syria. When its collapse seemed important only to Syrians, it concerned us little, but now our attention is riveted, as it has come to represent a much deeper civilizational decline. Syria has become a palimpsest of what might become of human civilization itself. Syria foreshadows a sort of civilizational apocalypse in which every backstop fails and the patient-world collapses. It is a scenario that looks increasingly likely in no small part due to the chaos that the conflict in Syria has fostered.

Syria is an inferno stoked of Western hypocrisy, Iranian cynicism, tyrannical psychopathy, and global ignorance. It is an abyss into which we all sometimes worry the world itself might someday slip. It is a wonder the way we sit watching: it can sometimes seem as if we are blind to the possibility of collapse. Never trust the worst is over; Syria is not some child's play but rather an epic-tragedy, and the worst may be yet to come.

THE IRONY OF
SYRIAN DISINTEGRATION

Syrians like to joke that Assad is just trying get the population back to where it was when he took office. The Syrian population grew by almost six million between 2000 and 2011, when his regime began slaughtering demonstrators. But since that time, four million have emigrated, and half a million have been killed, putting him well on the way to his goal. It is little wonder Syrian humor has become black, like thick Arabic coffee, whose grounds settle at the bottom of the cup. Syria is being reduced to rubble, with all too many Syrians crushed at the bottom. The resulting trauma is producing an array of coping mechanisms, from extremism to cynicism,[53] lending to Syria a sense of surreality.

Syria may be the first country to have entered postmodernity through the stone-age. The Syrian conflict is akin to the First World War in that while it involves virtually everyone, it is understood by seemingly no one. This lends to the conflict the impression of a war of all-against-all. Since everyone possible seems to be fighting, all-too many have concluded no one could possibly be right. But while war usually dirties everyone's hands, some will always be more sullied than others.

It was well understood in pre-war Syria that people could do what they wanted, so long as they did not discuss politics. The Assad regime made participation in communist parties punishable by lengthy jail sentences and membership in the Muslim Brotherhood punishable by death. Reporters Without Borders ranked it the world's fourth most censored press.[54] All of this made studying

Syria challenging. There have been few Syria experts to educate the press. And information on it has tended to be imperfect. Hence, when Assad blamed the peaceful protests that broke out in 2011 on "terrorists" and "foreign elements," few could confidently point out he was simply making it up.

It is ironic that while the effort to democratize Syria failed so miserably, the truth itself was so radically democratized. Where facts were hard to come by, hack-bloggers and conspiracy theorists simply took a cue from Assad and made them up. And as the conspiracy theories abounded, passive audiences became morally paralyzed. The more Syria was reduced to rubble, the more discourse on it came to dissolve into mud.

It was a classic postmodern case of moral authority being buried in a barrage of perspectives. But it was not simply the abundance of perspectives that made deciphering the truth so difficult. Leftist humanitarians stopped reading relatively impartial Amnesty International and Human Rights Watch reports in favor of Russia Today, blithely ignoring its reliance on mass political repression and journalist assassinations. If Syria was confusing, much of the reason lay in this reliance on censored state-media. But there was more.

The geopolitical changes transforming the Syrian landscape were tectonic. And as the ground moved, the left was caught flat-footed. American hegemony gave way in Syria to a multitude of would-be imperialists. Russia, Turkey, the Saudis, Iran. Meanwhile, anti-imperial activists fought the last war. Whereas Iraq began violently, Syria began nonviolently. Whereas Iraq was waged by a foreign power, Syrian protests were home-grown and from the ground-up. The left got Syria wrong, among other things, simply because their models did not match reality.

And whereas the right made things up in order to start a war in Iraq, the left made things up in order to stop a war in Syria. The Syrian left demonstrated for a better life, while the Western left defended regime war criminals against mainstream media criticism. The Syrian left organized for the right to express their views freely in a democratic society with equal rights for all, while the Western left organized to stop their own governments from protecting Syrians from mass starvation and chemical bombardment.

Leftists have long defended the marginalized and sought to bring about greater social equality, and they have almost always fought against imperialism. Hence, it is more than a little ironic that, in their confusion, the people who most cherished these goals often found themselves supporting some of the world's most conservative and imperialistic regimes. Leftist justice activists defended the neo-liberal Assad, to whom the Bush administration outsourced torture; the dictator Putin, who ended Russian democracy and made protesting virtually illegal; the Iranian mullahs, whose merger of church-and-state would have been too extreme for the most fanatical of American evangelicals. And it was all in the service of preventing a war few in the West were actually proposing. Somehow justice activists found themselves lauding dictators in suits, at whose hands they would almost certainly have been jailed and tortured. It was a moral degeneration in values rivaled today perhaps only by the rise of Trump.

Syria has become a factory that produces imperialists and anti-imperialists alike. But all too often the anti-imperialists cheer on the new imperialists, with far too little irony. Somehow the world's most absolutist dictators successfully pose as bastions of freedom against Western-inspired democracy. And the same people who rallied in support of Iran's Green Revolution and the Arab Spring reverse course to applaud the very dictators who shut them down.

Syria has since ancient times been a sort of vortex that draws in empires. The Greeks, the Romans, the Arabs, and the Ottomans all ruled Syria, but few called it home. And once again, a multitude of lesser-great-powers are sucked into this essentially poor, largely land-locked state, which was until quite recently considered to have little geo-strategic value. It is ironic this backwater is now a proving-ground for aspiring imperialists. It is ironic that so many bit players have so recently taken the global stage. It is ironic that somehow the black-hole has come to appear the center of the universe. And this abundance of ironies has leant to the global imaginary a sense of existential dread.

Syria has become the battleground on which the current world order is being torn apart, but it may also set the conditions for the coming order. And this is perhaps the greatest irony of all. To quote Psalms, "The stone that the builders rejected has now become the cornerstone." It remains to be seen the kind of international geopolitical order it will sustain.

THE SYRIANS WE FOUND
UNDER TURKISH CARPETS

The faces of the bathroom attendants fell when my girlfriend asked where they were from, for they had been mocking me behind my back and then realized she was fluent in Arabic. They apologized profusely but it was all water under the bridge when we realized they were Syrian refugees, just the people with whom we wanted to speak. And they had good reason to resent the Western tourists passing through the small town where they had settled.

Syrian refugees were being given papers and rights everywhere across Turkey, except for the tourist hotspot of Antalya, according to Ranya, a young teacher from Syria. It seems Turkey wanted to keep the refugees hidden from tourists and the attendees of an upcoming G-20 conference. Emerging states often go to extraordinary lengths to project the right appearance at such international events.

The last time my travels took me close to a G-8 conference in St. Petersburg, the usually colorless police had been asked to smile brightly, as if they were Americans at an amusement park. This time Turkey was sweeping it all under its gorgeous carpets, prepping the roads and making everything shine. If only the people attending these conferences had the depth to see through the mask to what truly matters.

Ranya had been a teacher in Syria, as were Hassan and his wife, with whom she was talking. But after three years in Turkey they could not find a school in which to educate their children. They had no papers and hence no access to government services. Their children could not be cared for in a hospital and the men were subject to arrest. But at least Ranya's husband was able to find work as a carpenter, and they had a decent place to live. Yet, it all came at the price of perpetual insecurity. They feared the slightest illness of their children, who would not be accepted in local hospitals. And while they might have opted to brave the journey to Europe, Hassan explained he had not yet felt so desperate as others to put his children at so great a risk.

"People say Assad or not Assad," explained Ranya, "but what we want is peace and security." That may well have been the case, but it might just as well have been the case they were afraid to talk, as the Assad regime rules through terror and their agents are rumored to be everywhere. Countless encounters with seemingly neutral Syrians, afraid of the consequences of taking a stand, have lent the impression to many observers that Assad is actually quite popular, when the truth is far murkier.

She explained that their house had been severely bombed shortly before they left Syria. And even as their eyes shined brightly, they all seemed to agree they had lost hope. They were hemmed in at every turn. They could get papers elsewhere in Turkey, and this would give them access to government services, but they would be unable to work and find a decent place to live. They could leave for Europe and find a better life, but the journey could mean the death of a child. They were divided about returning to Syria, though, with Ranya wanting to stay in Turkey and Hassan wanting eventually to go home.

The only hope lay in a negotiated settlement. And while it seemed to them the war would last forever, traumatic events often have this timeless quality. Whether sooner or later, the war in Syria will one day end. Soldiers are not unlike civilians in their tendency to grow war-weary: many a war has ended because the soldiers simply stopped showing up for work. Armies run out of supplies, leaders lose their nerves, external patrons cut off arms shipments, and sometimes the adults get together and decide enough-is-enough.

Former American President, Jimmy Carter, who has played a pivotal role in many democratic transitions the world over, has recently come out strongly in favor of a negotiated settlement. In an opinion piece in The New York Times, he notes that he has known Syrian President Bashar al-Assad since his time in college and believes he is an extremely rigid thinker who will fight to the end if there is no outside intervention. Carter has spoken with Russian President, Vladimir Putin, and says that he would accept a solution brokered by Russia, Turkey, Iran, Saudi Arabia, and the U.S. Under this scenario, Assad regime officials would need to have a seat in any transitional government to be followed by elections.[55] The devil would of course be in the details, with the big questions being the fate of the devil himself and how to protect against his officials seizing power in the transitional government. It may not be what the democracy protesters hoped for in 2011, but it would be a chance to bring some change.

It has become quite a typical ending to the great tragedies of our day. Few would have imagined such a fate awaiting Lebanon in the eighties or Bosnia in the nineties, where today we find corrupt but relatively reasonable democracies. Few would have expected Rwanda to become one of Africa's great growth miracles of the last generation. And no one would have predicted the appearance of the European Union, following the two world wars that devastated Europe in the twentieth century.

A little time spent with refugees can have a way of opening hearts and focusing minds. If Turkish leaders were smart they would not try to hide the Syrian refugees from the upcoming G-20 conference, for however much they may have obliterated their own democratic prospects, they have done an otherwise excellent job of caring for these misplaced persons. Rather, they would throw open the doors and invite them in for Turkish tea. Ranya and Hassan continually emphasized that they felt they had been forgotten by the world. If only they might be let in to tell their story perhaps the leaders would find the courage to step into the mix and put an end to the fighting in Syria and we could all forget them with a clean conscience. In the absence of such fantasies, the fighting wears on and the approaching winter seems as cold as ever.

CASABLANCA IN A SYRIAN CITY
OF SHIPPING CONTAINERS

Just after we left the refugee camp last night, a massive brawl broke out and four people were stabbed. They were sheltered in the office where we had been meeting that day and there were no serious injuries, but it was a reminder of the deep disturbances roiling beneath the surface. While we were told the vast majority of people in the camp were escaping either the Assad regime or Isis, there were nevertheless an array of ethnic groups living in close proximity and frustrations were running high.

The camp is just outside Athens, Greece, and it is a bit like Casablanca in a city of shipping containers. The refugees are well provided for with each person getting three meals a day, a small room to share in a box of a trailer, and a 90 Euro a month stipend. They even have access to a dock where much of the three thousand person community gathers in the evenings. But the camp is built on a giant empty lot void of life, and their food is often spoiled and contains cockroaches. The Athens heat is sweltering in the summer, and many have lost family and suffered immense traumas. Meanwhile, they wait endlessly to be accepted into Europe, unsure of which state they will be invited into and whether or not they will know anyone in their new home country. The stress that results makes of the camp a sort of powder keg. And yet the children laugh and play and the adults are friendly and respectful.

The resilience of the human spirit is simply astonishing.

Everyone complains of life in the camp, but as in the case of much communal living, social networks are strong and there are lots of smiles. It sometimes seems they will look back on this period of their lives as many soldiers look back on their time in the trenches, a time of intense bonds, deepened through shared traumas, and animated by close quarters. While that which does not kill us tends more often than not to leave us traumatized, it can also make us remarkably resilient.

An assortment of non-governmental organizations provide food and shelter and medical services. And while it is otherwise saintly work, the constant comings and goings of volunteers and refugees alike leaves most everything in chronic disarray. Given the conditions, it is a wonder anything gets done at all. Much like government services, aid groups perform some of the most difficult tasks, work which no one has yet found a way to make profitable. They work with the most troubled populations, a task that is never complete and often exhausting. And yet it is also deeply rewarding work – bringing dignity to the lives of others is itself dignifying.

My partner and I came to the camp to help refugees work through their trauma. What we found was an astoundingly resilient community of people, who were taking care of themselves. The school in which we are assisting emerged from the ground up, from the hands of Syrians and other refugees who teach the classes. A small Greek non-profit came to their assistance and now they are bringing educational services to hundreds of children. One of the teachers experienced so much bombing in Syria that he can only sleep a couple of hours a night. And yet, he is there each day helping the school grow.

The leader of the non-profit emphasizes the importance of respecting the work of refugees so that they might feel a greater sense of dignity, and of getting them out of the camps and integrated into Greek society. But at this stage, it is they who are welcoming us into their community and making us feel at home. Even with the violence and trauma, it is difficult not to come away with the feeling that whichever society takes in the highest proportion of them will come away the strongest.

Of course, there is a shadow side to everything, not least a massive community of traumatized people, run by an array of organizations, which is under-resourced and overburdened and whose membership is constantly changing. Aid workers are often strangely detached from the refugees and their organizations often appear dysfunctional. Most refugees with whom we speak say the Greek Navy, which oversees the camp, is stealing funds designated for food and outsourcing to a sub-par catering company.

The police outside the camp appear complacent and ignore violent outbreaks inside the camp. A significant portion of the police force in Greece are actually members of an unusually popular neo-Nazi party, so perhaps it is to be expected. But all of it adds to a sense of chaos and confusion that makes subtle psychological healing difficult. The former leadership coach and social entrepreneur in me longs to facilitate dialogue between the Greek authorities and the aid organizations, between the aid organizations and refugees, and between the leaders of different ethnic refugee communities.

But all of that fades into the background of a deeper process at work in the camp. Our own work is but a drop in the bucket, but we are part of a process, welcoming them into a new world. The refugees need to know that real people care about them, and they need to see their faces. They need to talk with people who are a part of the nations to which they will be immigrating, and they need to know we understand their plight. And in spite of the corruption, in spite of the conditions, someone needs to assure their most basic needs are being met. We will do our best to welcome them to Europe and the West mentally and emotionally resourced, with a sense of equality and care. It is a start to what will be a historic and epic journey we will all likely be hear about for the rest of our lives.

REFUGEES CAN TEACH
THE MEANING OF FREEDOM

Almost half of my family fled from the Iranian Revolution in 1979. Without the generous welcome granted by America and other Western countries, many might have died. The Iranian side of my family is Jewish, but they were targeted by the populist uprising with other Iranian elites. The uprising included large liberal and socialist contingents, but it was the most extreme religious fanatics who carried the day. And yet, the Muslim-Iranians who came to America to flee from the Muslim regime have since that time become perhaps the most prosperous ethnic minority in the country.

It was not the first time my family fled from a dangerous regime. My grandfather initially became a refugee from Iraq in World War I to escape conscription in the Ottoman army. The empire was falling to pieces at the time, and a nationalist uprising was committing genocide against its Armenians and ethnically cleansing its Greeks in an effort to create an ethnically pure heartland in the Anatolian Peninsula. Living on the outer margins of what would soon become Turkey, and part of a small ethnic minority, my grandfather would likely have been cannon fodder without the opportunity to immigrate to Iran.

Generations later, I would travel to the region to write about another genocide just getting started. A little known jihadist group had trapped up to 40,000 Yezidis, a tiny religious minority, on a small mountain range in northern Iraq, threatening to kill them if they did not convert to Islam. They were starving and dying of thirst and showing up in droves on the border between Iraq and Turkey, where I befriended several and wrote of their plight. All of them loved America and wanted to immigrate there so they could live freely and safely.

President Obama quickly sent in American airlifts, supported on the ground by a communist Kurdish militia that had up to that time been listed as a terrorist organization. Thus began the fight against the Islamic State. It may have been the first time in the modern era that a genocide was stopped cold by a humanitarian intervention just as it was getting started. But it was a war that would be fought less with weapons and more with the imagery and emotion of American tolerance.

There are many who would dismiss these horrors as par for the course when dealing with a so-called barbaric religion of violence like Islam. And yet, it was the Europeans who dragged the Ottomans into WWI, invented trench warfare and mowed each other down in the Battle of the Somme, killed off the bulk of Jews in WWII, took over the greater part of the world to rob it of its riches, and ultimately destabilized the Middle East for generations through its imperialism and support for secular dictators, all in the name of oil. Sometimes our comforts are built upon graveyards.

The God of the Muslims is the same God of the Christians and Jews—and the prophets of Judaism make up the vast bulk of Muslim prophets. Islam is known by its followers as the last of the three major Abrahamic faiths, though others like Baha'ism and Mormonism have followed. The spirit of Muslim scriptures is alive and well among its adherents, who have repeatedly demonstrated to me a vastly greater respect for my own religious beliefs than most Christians and Jews. It is one of the sad ironies fostered by an astonishingly ignorant media that the most religiously tolerant of the three major faiths has come to appear the most intolerant.

But the Middle East is a troubled part of the world, and it is bleeding refugees. My partner and I have interviewed and befriended many of them in Turkey, Lebanon, and Greece. And what we have continually found is bright and resilient individuals, who love their families and cherish their freedom, who want democracy and a better life. They are escaping unimaginable horrors and simply want to be given a chance to work and integrate into free societies where they can live safely and securely.

The Muslim ban so recently proposed by the Trump administration is grounded in an ignorance of their religion, fostered by prejudice against their cultures. It is the latest weapon in a war against their humanity, a contradiction of America's highest values, and a contravention of the American Constitution. It is also an inspiration to terrorists everywhere, who have welcomed its enactment. The ban tells Muslims they have no place in our society; that we are an inhumane people who cannot see their pain; that our tolerance is a façade, our riches skin deep, our institutions made for breaking.

The ban will tear apart families, subvert life trajectories, stop dreams short, and send countless individuals to their graves. These people are my friends and they might just as well have been my family. They often love our culture more than liberals and conservatives combined, because they know what true freedom means to the good life. They know that without the freedom to speak their minds they cannot form their thoughts and thus think for themselves – and that without the ability to organize with others for a better life, they are cursed to be bullied and exploited by leaders who care nothing for their fate.

The greatest irony of the ban is that it will foster the belief that freedom is an illusion, that tolerance is a privilege, and that politicians everywhere care only for their own petty selves. Donald Trump's inflated ego will stand as a symbol to them of every shattered dream and broken illusion they once associated with America. And the American dream will come to appear a little more like the nightmare of plutocratic populism.

Perhaps the saddest is irony is that while the ban is being done in the name of making America great again, it is saying to the world that America is merely ready to hate again – just as we did with the Irish and Italians, the Germans and the Jews, the Puerto Ricans and the Mexicans. Contrary to popular myth, Americans have long closed their hearts to refugees from famine and hardship, war and genocide. But while we have often given the cold shoulder to refugees, we have, over time, learned to tolerate their differences – and in tolerating their differences learned to appreciate their idiosyncrasies, and through appreciating their unique gifts integrated them in our great experiment in multicultural democracy. Syrians and Libyans, Iraqis and Yemenis all deserve this same chance at freedom, especially when the alternative is so often death.

WHY THE NEXT GENERATION
OF SYRIAN REFUGEES MAY THRIVE

We spent the day with Syrian refugees outside Athens. The camp is a giant parking lot surrounded by barbed wire fences. Its inhabitants have been bombed out and run from the places of their birth. They have lost loved ones at sea and shifted from camp to camp as they await the outcome of their fates. Some will go to Spain, some to Germany, some may be left to languish.

The camps are the front lines of the new global civilization. Here, Syrian Sunnis mingle with Iraqi Yezidis and Afghan Shias. Here, aid workers from Britain and France, Greece and America, struggle to meet their needs, while quietly and often unconsciously inducting them into the ways of the West.

It is common to think of cosmopolitan people as being wealthy, but the poverty of the refugees defies this assumption. It is often the poorest people in the world, who leave their own broken countries in search of a better life, who live in the most places, speak the most languages, and think the most globally.

The countries of the Levant – Lebanon, Palestine, Israel, Syria, and Greece – have long been known for their diversity. And they have often lain at the heart of trade routes. These places contain the flotsam and jetsam of Turkish, Persian, Greek, and Roman civilizations. They left their genes and disappeared. And now, like the Jews and Palestinians before them, a vast movement of peoples is being swept from this land. It is a tsunami that is transforming the world before our eyes.

Syrians would do well to look to the Palestinian diaspora as a model. Some may find this paradoxical, for no one is so bad off as the Palestinians – particularly the refugees in Lebanon and Syria. But we also find a Palestinian population that was displaced through war and ethnic cleansing and scattered across the world, which turned to education and benefitted from much international support. Palestinians have been the beneficiaries of a great deal of international aid, and their connections with activists and humanitarians have opened their minds and made of their diaspora one of the most cosmopolitan – at least the part of it lying outside the Middle East. It is sometimes said of Palestinians, as it is said of Indians, that they thrive everywhere but in Palestine.

But Syrians might also look to the Jews, the Greeks, or the Lebanese. Each of these groups was at one time or another pushed from the region – the Jews by force in ancient times, the Greeks by population pressures in the late nineteenth century, the Lebanese by conflict at the end of the twentieth century. But whatever the reasons for their emigration, each of these groups spread widely around the world and prospered.

Syrians will be scattered like the others before them, but whether they fall apart or flourish will depend greatly on the quality of support they receive in these camps. Whether they are able to integrate into the societies to which they are scattered will depend greatly on whether they are understood and treated with dignity. Whether they can get a leg up and live according to their own lights will depend greatly on whether or not they are supported.

Syrians themselves can take control of their fate by finding a deeper intercommunal meaning to their journeys. Sometime in the next few years, they will find themselves settling into their new home countries of Europe. They will be widely scattered, which means they will look to the comfort and support of other Syrians, whoever they supported in the war and whatever their ethnicity.

This unity will help in the rebuilding of Syria itself, and the Syrian diaspora may ultimately become a source of skilled professionals and business people, as well as politicians and peacemakers. The diaspora will most likely be better educated and wealthier than the Syrians back home, and their money and ideas will play a part in rebuilding the country.

The home country will need to draw upon their talents but to do so will have to accommodate their need for greater openness and voice. It is quite possible that, out of the spotlight of international news, a quiet revolution will take place in quest for their service similar to that played out between European monarchs and nobles in the opening of the first parliaments in the early modern era.

Whether or not Assad remains, they can push Syrian society to open up. They will be there in the background, exposing the corruption of Syrian officials in German and French newspapers, pressing for democratic freedoms in Danish non-profits, and arguing with Syrian officials whenever they leave the country. All of this can help Syrians to establish better and more inclusive institutions, whether or not Assad remains.

If the Syrian diaspora can remain unified, and work past its collective traumas, they can not only make Syria better than it was before the conflict, they can make it better than they had ever imagined. And while this may be a distant possibility, and while Syria might also become another North Korea, whose government also arose amid a thoroughly bombed out infrastructure, there are no shortage of countries that suffered a genocide and came out the better.

Perhaps Rwanda is the quintessential example. When the genocide was finally stopped, Rwanda was a broken and bankrupt country – 800,000 of whose citizens had just been hacked to death, two million of whose citizens had just fled in fear of retribution. But now it has rebuilt itself, becoming a model of African development, a relatively prosperous and stable state. While preparing for the worst, we should not dismiss the possibility of the best possible outcomes.

Syrians will no doubt need to discover their own model. And they would do well to look for leaders, whether at home or abroad, who can sustain a realistic vision of hope. Most importantly, they will need to recognize that they are playing a long game – and there is no telling where it may lead over the course of the next generation.

Finally, Syrians will be making their homes in a dizzying array of Western and Middle Eastern states. The breadth of their dispersal will probably lead them to integrate more quickly. And it will make them more likely to forge businesses across borders and to focus on the kind of higher education that can be taken wherever they go. Whether or not they can influence events back home, they may find themselves enriching their new homelands, where their youth and skills will be in demand.

Europeans and Americans would do well to envision some of these possibilities, but so also would Syrians themselves, who might better sustain hope with a vision and a dream, but whose visions and dreams will press the new rightwing nationalists to see them in another light. Beyond conservative prejudice and liberal compassion, the next generation of Syrians may thrive and strengthen our societies.

PART III

THE EMOTIONAL
LIFE OF ISRAEL

THE EMOTIONAL LIFE OF ISRAEL

He was a bestselling Israeli author, who had been deeply involved in the Israeli-Palestinian peace process as the former campaign manager of a left-labor Prime Minister. We were sitting in a café talking about what it means to live in a society pervaded by the sense of threat. Israel may possess one of the strongest militaries in the world, but people there often casually speak about being wiped out.[56] Much of this applied to his writings on evolutionary psychology.

But there was something subtler he wanted to convey. He was a successful businessman, and had some years back gotten involved in a socially responsible investment project in the West Bank. He wanted to support Palestinian development and was working closely with a local Palestinian businessman. But the man had somehow taken advantage of him – it was not clear how exactly – and it had broken his trust. He said he still gave to causes that other Israelis consider traitorous, and he was not making judgments on all Palestinians based on this one experience; he remained, in effect, relatively free from prejudice and quite sensitive. But it had somehow taken him out of the game.

The conflict with Palestinians is unusually personal for Israelis. Sometimes it can seem that everything revolves around questions of trust and persecution. All too many Israelis were run out of some country or other, or else they are the descendants of the survivors of genocide. While the Holocaust was unusually brutal, many of these other experiences were far more subtle,[57] more like a long series of hints that said in effect, you are not wanted, here is the door. And then there was the Palestinian terrorism, always in response to real injustices and almost entirely stopped since 2006, but lingering on in Israeli national consciousness like some childhood trauma that cannot be forgotten.

These experiences have lent to Israeli culture a collective sense of insecurity. Israel is a tiny country, in some places stretching a mere 13 miles east-to-west, and it is dominated by a rather small and unpopular minority. Hence, it is no surprise that Israelis tend to worry quite a lot about how the rest of the world views them. The insecurity is compensated for through an emphasis on military security and totalitarian control over the occupied territories. And with seemingly perfect anthropological symmetry, the totalitarian control provides young Israeli adults, suffering their own insecurities, as young adults so often do, the opportunity to play at being in command.[58] What better way to overcome your own insecurities, than to be given routine control over the intimate lives of others. It is the perfect mechanism for overcoming collective insecurity; unfortunately, it just leaves Israelis more disliked than ever, and hence collectively more insecure.

Criticize an Israeli's view of the occupation and you are likely to be met with the collective burden of generations of persecution. My own two-year relationship with a bright and spiritual, young Israeli woman decades ago was regularly punctuated with fights over the occupied territories. Sometimes they got so bad we would joke about having to call in Jimmy Carter. At the time, he was quite respected in Israel for his Camp David Peace Accords. But when he wrote a fairly moderate book focused on ending the occupation in 2006,[59] the American Israel lobby branded him an anti-Semite in a ruthless smear campaign.

Smearing critics as anti-Semites is quite common. But seldom do the supporters of Israel stop and think how this may strengthen the commitment of their critics. The Israel lobby has often gone after fairly neutral organizations, like Amnesty International and Human Rights Watch, for their alleged partiality. But in so doing they have made the conflict personal for activists, thereby inviting the collective wrath of justice and human rights advocates the world over. Overcompensation seems to pervade everything about the country.

Of course, the occupation is extremely personal for Palestinians, whose life prospects it has a tendency to cripple. And Israelis are often most personally affected by hearing how their policies personally affect Palestinians. Yet it is not the Palestinians feelings they tend to be concerned with but rather their own. It is as if their sensitivity has been displaced; the empathy they might otherwise feel for Palestinians is instead experienced as a sort of personal injury. It is much like the person who is more concerned with the rude manner with which some injustice has been presented than the injustice itself.

While the sensitivity of Israelis may be most evident in the vicious manner in which emotion is used to manipulate critics today, this range of feelings and emotional engagement has often produced stunningly subtle works of literature and philosophy. Twentieth century Jewry produced thinkers like Theodore Adorno, Gertrude Stein, Jacques Derrida, Sigmund Freud, Hannah Arendt, Franz Kafka and Albert Einstein. And Israel has produced two world class novelists in David Grossman and Amoz Oz, who have themselves struggled with the meaning of the occupation.[60] These are innovative and subtle thinkers, known for crossing boundaries between disciplines, and for their incisive psychosocial insights. Together, they display a striking degree of emotional intelligence that has enriched Western culture and global civilization.

But the Jewish use of emotional intelligence today has been distorted. And the manipulation of the emotional lives of critics has reached crisis proportions.[61] Israelis do not seem to understand the resentments their actions perpetuate and the violent reactions they sometimes inspire. And they seem increasingly detached from a deeper Jewish tradition in which this emotional sensitivity is explored through the interplay between the conscious and unconscious, self and other, us and them – as exemplified by so many of their culture's greatest thinkers. It is a far more cosmopolitan tradition, a tradition more likely to draw from the thinking of those whom Israelis now oppress, and to generate a multicultural vision of inter-ethnic harmony. There have been stranger turns in the life of Jewish culture, and it can increasingly appear that without such a transformation, Jewish culture will itself become the victim of its own overzealous guardians.

THE LONG DECLINE
OF ISRAELI SOCIALISM

Kibbutz Negeb was set up in the middle of three Palestinian villages in 1942, so as to more easily organize Arab workers and
build an Israeli worker-state with equal rights for all. Legend has
it that the twentieth-century Jewish settlement of Israel occurred
primarily through the Kibbutzim, small communes laced throughout the countryside, but most Jews moved to the cities when they
first arrived in Palestine.[62] Some of the most prominent Jewish
intellectuals of the twentieth century, like the philosopher Martin
Buber, and the Kabbalist Gershom Scholem, supported something
like today's "one-state solution," which would see Jews and Arabs
granted equal civil and political rights in Israel and its occupied
territories.[63] But the ideal disappeared with the founding of Israel
in 1948, when over 650,000 Palestinians were ethnically cleansed
from the state.[64]

The history of Kibbutz Negeb is related to me by Avshalom
Vilan, a friend and former leader of the Israeli socialist party. The
Mapam Party he headed for some time was a major political party
when Israel was founded, but it is now defunct. It is much the same
with the Kibbutz movement in general, which was until recently
core to the Israeli political system. Abu, as his friends call him,
suggests the decline of the Kibbutzim and his party are closely
related to that of the Israeli state itself. He obsesses over how to
end the occupation through a two-state solution and make Israel
a normal, Western democracy. Israel is changing fast and he is
deeply worried.

Abu was a co-founder of Peace Now, which has worked to de-militarize Israeli society, starting in the late seventies, and he has spent the last few decades working for a two-state solution. He served in Israel's Parliament, the Knesset, and sat on the finance committee, where he and others sought to uncover how the settle-ments were funded, but to no avail. Both Palestinian-Israeli activists and center-left Meretz Party members with whom I spoke in Israel hold him in high regard.

He proudly relates how, until about 10 years ago, all property in his Kibbutz was held in common, but it has since that time been largely privatized. And he suggests the privatization of the Kibbutz mirrors that of Israeli society more generally. He clearly loves the Kibbutz, which his father founded. Yet, however strongly his moral decency shines through and however easy it is to empathize with his visions, it is all too closely associated in my mind with a state whose war crimes and occupation leave me cold. And this is also part of the decline about which he speaks. For progressive Jews used to embrace Israel and fight to make it better and more just, whereas now they tend to fight against it in the name of justice.

Twentieth-century Zionism was a racist and nationalist ideol-ogy,[65] but it was also a visionary socialist ideal.[66] Abu's narrative suggests things could have turned out differently. He points out that, while accounting for only about 3 percent of the society, until quite recently Kibbutz members held 10 percent of the seats in Israel's Knesset and exercised an outsized role. For the Kibbutzim were core to the society and its members were the cream of the crop. This core group was mostly secular, socialist, and European in origins. Their vision for Israeli society was quite different from what all too often appears a highly unequal and racist state today. But to a rela-tive outsider, more concerned with justice for Palestinians, it does not appear as different as Abu might like to believe.

The occupation of Gaza and the West Bank, which began in 1967,[67] was initiated by these Ashkenazi, or European, Jews. However, it is a matter over which they have always been torn.[68] The Mizrahi, or Middle Eastern Jews, who began flocking to Israel in ever-greater numbers in the sixties and seventies, were often more capitalistic and prejudiced against Muslims, due to the discrimination they faced in Muslim societies, and they were also more comfortable with the occupation and colonization of Palestinian lands.[69] This is at least part of the reason they have faced discrimination at the hands of fellow Israelis. They overcame their marginality in the late seventies and began to lead governments, though. And this split Israel at the core.

There is an oft noted pecking order to Israeli society. The Ashkenazi Jews sit at the top. The Middle-Eastern, Mizrahi, come next, followed by the Russian Jews, who began to arrive in the late eighties with the Ethiopians, who among the Jews at least sit at the bottom. These are followed in descent by Palestinian-Israelis, occupied Palestinians, and finally the Bedouin. It is a highly stratified and tense social system, with a fluid multi-party, semi-inclusive democracy, which is prone to breakdown. Internal tensions are often exacerbated by external conflicts and then projected outward onto marginal groups. As in many states, social inequality is a partner to imperialism.

Just as Israelis began to take the prospect of a Palestinian state seriously in the nineties, the pace of colonizing the West Bank quickened.[70] Meanwhile, their own society was fracturing into a series of separate racial and ethnic groups. The Ultra-Orthodox were also populating rapidly, and Palestinians within Israel were beginning to feel disaffected, after decades of failed integration. Then the economic inequality of the early 2000's struck,[71] along with the Second Intifada, a Palestinian uprising involving extensive terror attacks, after which support for the left-labor coalition plummeted – and Israel became a sort of falling star.

Kibbutz Negeb, along with Kibbutzim more generally, began to experience difficulties around this time as well. In order to retain members they had to offer greater freedom and the ability to keep more personal earnings. They also began to lose representatives like Abu in the Knesset. By the time of my arrival, Kibbutz Negeb still had some thriving businesses and a dairy, but it was beginning to sell off many of its assets and it had about it the sense of a ghost town.

All of this bodes ill for those hoping for a Palestinian state or a single democratic state with equal rights for all. The conservative demographic is growing while the progressive-socialist demographic is declining. One former left-labor campaign manager of an Israeli Prime Minister spoke to me of there being no hope that the left would achieve power in the foreseeable future. Until there is a deeper integration of Israeli society, there is always the danger it will continue to project its problems outward onto the Palestinians, which will fuel conflict and insecurity in a vicious circle. Further, the demographic disintegration of Israeli society makes it easier to blur boundaries, which has made settlement building easier to slip by those who might otherwise raise red flags.

Readers may sense in this narrative a hint of the elegiac. It is a narrative of decline that is often heard among Israel's left.[72] The narrative is a kind of creed for those Israelis who are most dedicated to building a just and equal society. It differs from Palestinian narratives, which tend to be much sadder and harsher,[73] but it is similar insofar as both tend to yield few good answers. Whether Palestinians win their own state or they later become equal members within a shared democratic state, they will need to be able to relate to their most natural allies within Israel.

Both groups will need to stop seeing past each other if peace for Israelis, and peace and justice for Palestinians, is ever to be achieved. It would help greatly if they could begin to tell stories of their common decline. Out of those stories might emerge newer narratives for a better shared future. This will take a lot of listening on both sides, and there will be much frustration and dissatisfaction along the way. Israelis will want to assert that their suffering is equivalent to that of Palestinians, and Palestinians will often want to give up.

But this work, which is often derided by Palestinians and their supporters as "normalization" of the occupation, serves a political purpose for both sides. Palestinians need to tell Israelis their stories if they are to win support, which barring military victory, will be necessary to any solution. And Israelis need to live up to their own democratic, secular ideals if they are to stave off the moral decline and isolation of their society. It will be difficult, but few great struggles are easy.

THE PARADOX OF
PALESTINIAN CULTURE

The guy was big and tough looking – just at that age when young men are most prone to beating up people they do not know, and he was standing there with two grumpy looking friends. Palestine felt remarkably safe but it is not the kind of place where you want to try your luck. It was late and getting dark. And the small neighborhood in the heart of Bethlehem was starting to look a little rough, not to mention that a shopkeeper had just told me to be careful.

I tried to avoid eye contact for the most part, but as they walked by, I nodded a gentle smile and the big guy asked, "Where are you from?" I said "America," but I might as well have said, "the country whose media has made you look like a terrorist and diminished your life prospects through tacit support for the Israeli occupation." Not a moment passed before he stuck out his hand and smiles appeared all around. And then said in that warm and welcoming tone of Mr. Rourke from Fantasy Island, "Welcome, welcome to Bethlehem," and everyone shook my hand.

The word Palestinian has been criminalized in the minds of most Americans. It is often associated with irrationality and terror- ism. Palestinians in the West Bank have been under Israeli occupa- tion for almost half a century. They have been ruled by military de- cree, and their lands have slowly been confiscated and colonized.[74] Their movement is stifled by checkpoints,[75] and houses are often demolished for political activity. Their relationships are broken by informers to whom Israeli authorities promise the rewards of free- dom, and peaceful protesters are often shot. [76] Hence, resistance tends to be driven underground, and the whole culture takes on the appearance of criminality.

But while the Palestinians in the West Bank showed me hard exteriors, they also exhibited warm interiors. The closer you get, the warmer the welcome. Everyone was giving me coffee and sweets, extra food and discounts on rooms. It was often confusing as to which gifts were free and which came with an expectation of reciprocity, for it seemed a deeply ingrained sense of kindness. But it lent to the experience a warm glow of welcome from a culture vastly exceeding my highest expectations. My observations are far from unique: this is what it appears most people coming to Palestine have to say.

Reporters in the West seem to miss this kindness, though. Reporters tend to stay in pricey hotels and usually cover political drama, not day-to-day life. They also come with their own prejudices, ingrained through focusing only on the violence. They must speak to the prejudices of their Western audiences, and focusing on the violence, they come to see more of it. Meanwhile, audiences in the West tend to see only the worst parts of Arab culture, turning their ephemeral ideas into concrete facts in the mind. Poorly educated in this foreign culture, they then string together misplaced verses from the Qur'an, speculations of media pundits, pieces of pro-Israeli propaganda, and confused readings of Christian history, into some vision of a clash of civilizations. But the picture they create is a cartoonish caricature.

The sense of honor among Palestinians is strong, to be sure. And it accounts for the strength of the Palestinian resistance. I am told you can dishonor a man by looking the wrong way at his wife, by injuring a member of his tribe, and perhaps most importantly for Israel, by stealing his land. When you cross these lines of honor, the aggression can be intense. Palestinian culture thus seems largely passive and warm, with the capacity for aggression should the kindness be taken for granted and the people dishonored.

There is also something surprisingly moderate about Palestinian culture. Palestinians do not debate much and often yield to opposing views. This lends to conversation a fluid flexibility that one does not find in the Jewish and American supporters of Palestinians. Those in the West Bank constantly sought to make their acceptance of my partial Jewish heritage clear. Even though it is not an important part of my own identity, and some were even atheists, they bent over backwards to show respect. It is the same moderation shown to me by Muslims the world over.

But it can often seem a highly formal and traditional sort of moderation. And it appears to stretch into romance as well, where Palestinian friends have told me the formalism can be heartbreaking and confusing. Under better circumstances, this formalism might result in the sort of everyday pressures that are part of life in any complex society. But coupled with the frustrations of daily life under occupation and the accompanying economic underdevelopment, it is easy to imagine how such pressures might become explosive.

These are speculations, to be sure, as they must be. For there is simply too much going on in any given culture for even its own members to sum it up in such broad and sweeping strokes. But such speculations can open a window of understanding where before we had only a media constructed hall of mirrors. We need to look less to the violence and more to everyday living. Otherwise we will miss the thousand little disagreements among Palestinians, which if we would only listen might signal a space for dialogue. And we will miss the open arms with which we might be greeted if only we would share in the sharing.

So many Palestinians want to open their homes and touch something of that ever-tarnished but still shining American magic. When we fail to take up the offer, we lose something of our own humanity in the process, failing to grasp the way human goodness shows up everywhere, and in the process dishonoring them for their kindness.

As the rise and fall of tensions in Israel and Palestine repeat themselves like some myth of the eternal return, we would do well to pause and look deeper. Much is lost when we fail to respect the ordinary dignity of Palestinians. They will resist in whatever way they can, Israel will be less secure, and America will be continually drawn into the Middle East. A warm handshake and a smile might not stop a needless war and end the occupation, but it is a start to making peace and forging the kind of security that will allow all of us to see more deeply into one another's hearts.

THROWING STONES FROM
OCCUPIED PALESTINE

The donkey-cart was racing in circles through the streets of Hebron in front of Israeli soldiers, who were gathering for a fight. Palestinian youths drew together just down the street, picking up numbers before beginning another ritualized act of stone-throwing. It was just outside the old marketplace of Hebron, perhaps the most fought over stretch of territory in the Palestinian West Bank.

Several hundred Israeli religious-extremists plunked a colony smack-dab-in-the-middle of the main Hebron market several decades back and have terrorized the locals ever since. The settlers are there to reclaim land taken from a few dozen Jews killed in a pogrom in the early-thirties and to fulfill a religious mission. And their presence has destroyed the marketplace and much of the life of this city of nearly a quarter-million. International observers attest that they regularly drop trash and liquids on the heads of Palestinian passersby from upper-level apartments, and it has gotten so bad that shopkeepers have had to cover the market with a mesh-wire fence that periodically fills with trash.[77]

An Israeli soldier stationed in Hebron told me the role of the Israeli Defense Forces there is to keep the peace between extremists on both sides. Ask Israeli soldiers and police in Palestinian territories what they are doing there and you will hear a similar refrain. But the abuses and humiliations of Palestinians regularly occur in Hebron without intervention, as Israeli soldiers look on. There is even a guard tower in the middle of the market, where shopkeepers say the IDF sits watching as settlers harass the locals. Countless vid-

eos of young Palestinian schoolchildren being stoned by settlers, as
international aid workers escort them to school, tell a similar story.

The soldier spoke of his job proudly, amid my gentle fusillade
of questions. Why defend these fanatics who only cause trouble for
your state? Why spend hour-after-hour, day-after-day, in the hot sun,
in order to defend an occupation that is inherently unjust? Why not
travel and see the world or help people who really need it? His answers reminded me of corporate employees who go to outrageous
lengths to defend the injustices of their employers; his trembling
handshake betrayed an inner lack of confidence.

There was good reason for the stone-throwing boys to want
to run the soldiers out. The Israelis were the occupying power and
had just begun an incursion into the city. Soldiers can easily protect themselves from stone-throwers but periodically shoot to kill.
Throwing stones can be dangerous business and it must take incredible courage and commitment to daily play Palestinian David to the
Israeli Goliath. As if to highlight the dangers, my good friend and
guide to the action, who was from a nearby village, noted he had
been shot in a nonviolent verbal encounter with settlers in his youth.

And yet, it all seemed so casual and routine. A Palestinian fruit-
seller, who was quickly packing his goods, had even set up shop
in the middle of the melee. The donkey-cart taunts and the blind-
massing of soldiers made the stone-throwing appear less an act of
just retribution and more just a ritualized dance of trauma. When
asked about the role of the IDF, he said most do work to keep the
peace, but they also favor the settlers. The problem is the occasional
fanatic, who shoots to kill and goes unprosecuted.

The occupation of Palestinian territories compounds the collective traumas inflicted on Palestinians and Israelis alike. Military occupations are inherently violent, and violence can be magnetizing.
The presence of the settlers in Hebron was wholly unnecessary, as
were their soldier-protectors. But the stone-throwers also seemed to
be doing little good. And if my friend was correct, local Palestinians
did not hold them in the same high-esteem international activists do.

The addiction to the adrenaline of danger, the ritualized reenactment of mutually-assured-destruction, and the hypnotic draw of action are all intensified by trauma.[78] The urge to obliterate one-self, the inability to step-back and assess, and role reversals between victims, perpetrators, and observers are also intensified. The sense of connectivity and immersion in the moment can be highly addictive. [79] And perhaps these experiences are triggered in some special way by the infusion of religiosity, which deepens communal bonds and permeates the land. Through religion the whole world has been drawn into Israel and Palestine, lending to it an outsized role in the world, perhaps best summarized by my Argentinian friend whose befuddled college roommate thought tiny Israel was actually bigger than their own massive country.

Watching such ritualized re-enactments of trauma can be like staring into a whirlpool. The violence is exciting and mesmerizing. Observers tend to tack back-and-forth between being pulled-in and wanting to run. The trauma specialist, Peter Levine, recommends that both urges should be resisted. He argues instead for standing in the middle of the trauma and letting it wash over your feet.[80] But the sense of being caught up in a great historical struggle can be energizing. We stand in solidarity with the stone-throwers, hearts pounding and adrenaline coursing through our veins, neglecting more elegant solutions. The problem with violence is that it tends to provoke more violence.

It has become almost a cliché in some Palestinian circles to say they are waiting for their Gandhi. However justified the violent re-sistance to occupation may be, the world might run to someone who could reason through the issues, without denying the injustices and the suffering on both sides, and yet speak directly to the criminality inherent in the Israeli occupation, forging a nonviolent resistance that would finally put it to rest.

I tried to stand in the middle and see all sides while exposing the inherent injustice of the occupation. I believed decades of medi-tation and years of studying genocide and ethnic cleansing would immunize me to addictive traumatic re-enactments. But one night of bombings set me on edge and just a few weeks of it made a wreck of my life. Another year-and-a-half of activism suffused my days with anxiety. I watched as activist colleagues became increasingly extreme in their views and members of the movement to end the occupation fell out among themselves. Everyone seemed to be on their own wild-donkey rides and spinning out of control.

These reflections lay dormant in my mind while waiting to catch a glimpse of the stone-throwing, as if everything to come was foretold in the actions of the stone throwers themselves. An observer of victims-taunting-perpetrators, I became part of the dance, like you the reader and the news reporters to whom you listen. Stone-throwers and soldiers, activists and readers, writers and escapists are all part of this dance. We are all grappling with how to respond to collective trauma and injustice from which it springs. The wrong reactions can breed more conflict, more injustice, and more trauma in an endless cycle of suffering. It is time we learn to view it all from a more mature vantage and break the cycle once-and-for-all.

THE GERMANS KILLED THE JEWS
AND THE JEWS KILLED THE ARABS

Sometimes you simply cannot make it up. I was looking out the window of a little hippy cafe in Kathmandu in the early nineties, passing the time between meditation courses, when all of a sudden a small boy was smacked by a larger boy, who was immediately smacked by a still larger boy, who was in turn smacked by their mom. It was all like dominoes, and that is the way the world should work, with the little guy protected at every stage by someone higher up.

But usually the chain runs in the opposite direction, with the proverbial boss yelling at his employee, who hits his wife, who smacks her son, who kicks the dog, which bites the mailman. People who have been abused want to get back at the perpetrators of their abuse but usually lack the ability, so they transfer their aggression onto someone more defenseless, who does the same to another on down the line. And so the cycle of violence ripples forth from one group to another, as outsiders caught in the crossfire are gradually transformed into insiders, like some barroom brawl that never ends.

The cycle of violence between Arabs and Jews is not usually portrayed this way. Rather, it is imagined as being much more tribal, with one side having to exact revenge for the actions of the other, back and forth like an eternal game of ping-pong. But the conflict often seems a lot more like this transference, perhaps best summarized in a Roger Waters song from the eighties, *"And the Germans kill the Jews, and the Jews kill the Arabs, and the Arabs kill the hostages, and that is the news."*

Holocaust trauma is passed down through both familial pathologies and political indoctrination in Israel. The Holocaust looms large with the ghost of Hitler outsized and ever-present. Israelis want to stand up to Hitler, but he is long dead, so they have to find someone else upon whom they might transfer their loathing,[81] and Hamas has come to play stand-in. Thus, Israel does to Hamas what it really wants to do to a long dead madman who stalks their fantasies of revenge.

Transference seems to lurk around every corner of the imagination in the Holy Land. Palestinians can look a lot like the new Jews. They are a progressive, highly educated, stateless people, skilled at business, scattered across the world, and abused by a ruthless power. And they are the victims par excellence, not only helpless but easily defensible. Supporters of Palestinians have latched onto this victimhood and in the process drawn to their ranks some of the world's most bullied activists, who transfer their own sense of victimization onto the Palestinians. If you want to stand up to your own autocratic or corrupt government but lack the means, or you want to stand up to the childhood bully who is no longer around, you can redeem yourself by standing up to Israel instead.

Perhaps this is quite common in social justice causes, but it is also quite dysfunctional.

The suppression of political rights in the Arab world and Israel's existence as one of but a handful of outright colonial powers left in the world, makes Israel an unusually good target upon which to unleash one's suppressed desire for justice. The only problem is this risks concretizing the Palestinian role of pure victim, the Israeli role of complete perpetrator, and the activist role of unmitigated hero. This is dangerous, because while Palestinians are truly victims and the Israelis perpetrators, each contains a little of the other – and activists are notorious for possessing their own agendas.

Through concretizing what are actually far more fluid roles, we excuse the abuses of the one side and fail to notice opportunities to transform the other. Thus, we turn victims and perpetrators alike into caricatures of themselves. But since these caricatures serve a purpose for each respective group, the outside supporters who reinforce them often simply make Israelis into more thorough perpetrators and Palestinians into better victims. Meanwhile, both groups vie for the status of victim, while they are treated by the other as the ultimate perpetrator.

It is a classic drama triangle, replete with all of the anxieties and neuroses typical of such relational distortions.[82]

Much of what Israelis attribute to Palestinians seems pure projection. In other words, they imagine Palestinians doing all the things they themselves are doing but cannot face. While Israelis regularly complain about Hamas using metaphorical human shields, Human Rights Watch and Amnesty International[83] have repeatedly disputed the veracity of these claims.[84] Hamas has certainly fired rockets from heavily populated areas – Gaza is one of the most populated places in the world, after all. And it is quite possible that they have done so intentionally on a handful of occasions. But Israeli Defense Forces have been found on multiple occasions to literally grab Palestinians and shield their own bodies with those of the Palestinians, who are often children.[85] Meanwhile, they complain of Hamas killing civilians, while it is they who kill the vast majority; they complain of Palestinian racism when theirs has been repeatedly demonstrated to be stronger.

Israelis see themselves as the true victims, but the victimization upon which they fixate has transformed them into perpetrators. In finding a stand-in for the Nazis whom they themselves can abuse, Israelis have come to play the same abusive role as the Nazis. Of course, to say they are playing the same role is not to say they are as murderous as the Nazis–that would be hyperbolic. Rather they are playing a role they learned from the Nazis, complete with racial identity cards and Palestinian ghettoes, imprisoned populations and their own militarized society. The role reversal is tragic, as much a cause for sympathy as outrage, and all quite normal behavior for victims, who quite typically come to play the role of their abusers in later life. But while it may be tragic and while highlighting it may often sound offensive, addressing it may be necessary for peace.

The whole psycho-drama is sustained by the collusion of passive observers who have been cowed into silence. What is actually happening is quite simple. A formerly abused minority is carrying out a military occupation of another people who they themselves must now abuse in order to sustain the colonization of their land. Were this to occur anywhere else in the world, the dynamics of the conflict might be much the same. The occupied people would resist, sometimes peacefully, more often with violence, as extremism took root among them and the international community called for an end to the occupation. Meanwhile, the occupying power would become increasingly militarized and brutish, as their culture came to justify and explain away its abuses of power. This is not tribal violence but colonialism, and that is a problem for which the solution is quite simple.

The occupation fuels the psycho-drama by perpetuating the tensions that lend the trance strength. Were the occupation to end, the psycho-drama might simply vanish into thin air. The hall of mirrors might come crashing down when the occupation ends, because even though the psychological complexes are real and may last for some time, they are sustained by the sense of threat that is a result of the occupation. Israelis feel threatened by Palestinians, who they themselves have threatened, leaving both groups in a perpetual state of threat. The occupation is thus like a drug that sets the madness in motion. Just end the occupation and with it much of the madness itself will end.

NETANYAHU'S TRANSUBSTANTIATION OF HOLOCAUST GUILT

The Israeli Prime Minister, Benyamin Netanyahu recently claimed that Hitler did not want to exterminate the Jews until he was convinced to do so by the Palestinian Grand Mufti, Amin Husseini. The Grand Mufti was the cleric overseeing Islam's holy places in Jerusalem and was perhaps the most powerful Palestinian under British rule. But the most powerful Palestinian under British rule was a mere peon compared with the world's most powerful dictator. Given the relative power differential between Hitler and Husseini, the minimal contact between them, and the fact that Hitler's animus toward the Jews preceded the Holocaust by decades, the statement is a bit absurd.

His claim may seem a harmless piece of propaganda by an unusually ham handed leader, but Netanyahu's claim is actually a form of Holocaust denial. Just as in other forms of Holocaust denial, Netanyahu shapes the Holocaust to suit his own political agenda. And just as in other forms of Holocaust denial, his statement will be used by neo-Nazis in the service of anti-Semitic fascism. This transference of Holocaust guilt from the Germans to the Palestinians accomplishes numerous other goals as well.

By blaming a Palestinian leader for the Holocaust, Netanyahu transubstantiates Holocaust guilt. As if by some act of magic, the high priest of Israeli mystification transfers blame for the Holocaust from the Germans to the Palestinians. No longer are we to blame the Germans, who are now a reliable Israeli ally, but rather the Palestinian puppet-master, who acted behind the scenes to shape the will of Hitler, even after the Palestinians had been thoroughly disarmed by Britain following their failed uprising in 1936.[86]

Israelis have long substituted Palestinians for Germans in their fantasies of collective revenge.

While the Holocaust is often used as an excuse for Israeli collective violence, Israeli collective traumas are real enough. The fear of existential annihilation is palpable in conversations among Israelis. It is the result of thousands of years of persecution, an unusually thorough genocide at the hands of the Third Reich, generations of warfare with various Arab states, and decades of Palestinian terrorism, which was almost entirely halted in 2006. It affects Israeli psychology, social organization, and military mobilization. But now that the Israeli military is one of the most powerful in the world, the victim has been turned to perpetrator, killing Palestinian civilians at a ratio of about 100-to-1 in recent conflicts,[87] and this sits uncomfortably with Israelis.

If the Germans are responsible for the Holocaust, then Israel is simply being a bully to innocent Palestinians who had nothing to do with it. But if the most powerful Palestinian at the time of the Holocaust could be held responsible for it, then Israel is doubly absolved. First, Israel is absolved of its perpetration of collective violence against Palestinians, for Israel is simply avenging itself for the Holocaust. Second, Israel is absolved of its inferiority complex brought on by the Holocaust, for Israel is now beating up the bully, which caused the death of six million Jews. All of a sudden, the Israeli victim-turned-perpetrator is absolved of both its inferiority before the European bully and its sadism over the Palestinian victim. And this lays the groundwork for a very real Israeli genocide against Palestinians in the future.

But if we are to blame the Grand Mufti for the Holocaust, two more miracles are also accomplished. Anti-Semitic fantasies have long seen Jews pulling the strings of great world events. But now it is the Palestinians who are pulling the strings. If Palestinian puppet-masters can control even Hitler at the prime of his power, then Palestinians might take on the role of the new Jews in the minds of conspiracy theorists. Like the Jews prior to the formation of the state of Israel, Palestinians are displaced across a wide diaspora, increasingly successful, well-educated, and the victims of great prejudice. But now with this new mystification of Holocaust guilt, they have become heirs to the secret society of Rothschilds and the Illuminati.

If Palestinians can be held responsible for the Holocaust, the relationship of the Jews to Europe will also be healed. By holding Muslims responsible for perhaps the worst event to ever befall the continent, the Holocaust becomes simply a dumb mistake. While it often appears as if Muslims have taken over the role of despised European minority previously held by Jews, holding a Muslim responsible for removing the Jews from Europe demonstrates that Israelis belong in Europe. They are part of the European family, living in a civilized democracy, and now the Muslims are the ones who must be cleansed. But if the Muslims who must now be cleansed from Europe, then who but the arch enemy of Muslims the world over would make the most reliable ally?

The most brutal leaders are commonly the most dishonest. Each lie further implicates their followers in their crimes and raises the bar on any efforts to defend their actions. This tightens the ranks of their followers, who with every lie enter more deeply into a world of myth. But the lies also staunch the moral fervor of would-be critics, whose own supporters are left stumbling after every lie. If you do not know who the Mufti is – however insignificant he may be in actuality – how can you say anything about his influence over Hitler? And if you cannot say who concocted the idea of the Holocaust – in spite of the fact that Hitler considered killing off the Jews in his writings as early as 1923 – who are you to speak out on the affairs of its victims?

This effort to play at being the expert on everything from the "Arab mind" to the true causes of the Holocaust, as a means of shutting down critics, is a common tactic of Israel's supporters. And it is quite possible that Netanyahu was being less deceptive and more the victim of his own unconscious fantasies in his outrageous claims this time. But as Israel strives with every act of imagined propaganda, to make itself appear a prosperous and stable democracy, deserving of entry into the club of civilized nations, it sets for itself a bar it can never reach without sweeping changes to every element of its society and government. The more Israel suggests it belongs in Europe, the more Netanyahu looks like Assad, and with that perception a whole new set of insecurities suffuses Israel's bad conscience—not least, the insecurity that their leader looks ridiculous in the eyes of the world.

THE NEW JEWISH PROPHETS

As the state of Israel shows the worst face of the Jewish tradition, and anti-Semitism peaks its head from the dark crevices of the European collective unconscious, Jews would do well to set the best parts of Judaism against the worst and to celebrate the Jewish embrace of justice and diversity.

Perhaps the worst anti-Semites of today are the Israeli leaders who justify their abuse of Palestinians in the name of the Jewish people. This is a categorical confusion whose results might be devastating. For if challenging Israel is equated with being anti-Semitic, and the phrase is repeated like a scratched record skipping, the enemies of Israel may find themselves slipping into thinking of themselves as the enemies of the Jews. And thus, frustrations with Israel may get mixed in with an older tradition of rightwing anti-Semitism. The dangers are particularly high in an era in which rightwing populists and fascists are growing in strength in every part of the world.

The Jews have long been an ethnically exclusive yet cosmopolitan minority, simultaneously mercantile and socialistic, rigidly learned and eccentrically brilliant.[88] Jews can be a colorful bunch, falling into no easy categories—Franz Kafka and Gertrude Stein, Karl Marx and George Soros, Sigmund Freud and Albert Einstein. And it has been quite common for people on the right to respond to these ambiguities with a queasy sort of repulsion. For Jews challenge what it means to be an insider to the nation.[89] But Jews have often been mistrusted by many on the left as well, who see them as capitalist elites with too much power, a privileged minority with no allegiance to the people.[90] The slide toward militaristic fascism in Israel complicates this ambiguity, for it highlights the most ethnocentric elements of Jewish culture. And this says to the right that Jews cannot be trusted as insiders and to the left that they cannot be trusted with power.

Judaism is the oldest and, at the core of its scriptures, arguably the most ethnocentric of the major world religions. God commands the Jews to commit genocide against other peoples no less than five times in the Torah so that they might take the Promised Land. These divine decrees were reinterpreted in the Jewish Talmud and are rarely taken at face value, but they matter in that they inspire much of the Israeli colonization of the West Bank today. It is a project that has been with the Jews since ancient times, when God placed them above other peoples and promised to protect them in exchange for their allegiance. The link cannot be clearer to anyone who has actually taken the time to read the Torah.

But like the Western philosophical tradition, Judaism is more a series of arguments than positions. Judaism is more often than not a dialectic of scriptural interpretations, summarized in lengthy treatises like the Talmud. Jews argue with God, they argue with one another, and they argue with their own traditions. The Jews who have challenged the injustices of their own state and people have in fact often been granted a special place, after their deaths, at the center of the Jewish tradition.

Were they alive today, it does not seem too far fetched to imagine many of the prophets of the Hebrew Bible raging against the occupation and the deliberate attack on civilians in Gaza. After all, a substantial portion of Jewish scriptures consist of Jewish prophets railing against their own people for their ethical lapses. Any serious perusal of Jewish history reveals a constant stream of such prophets and intellectuals, visionaries and reformers, pressing their people to be better. Jewish reformers have been arguing with their people for their moral lapses from ancient times through modernity and into postmodernity, and the arguments enriched the culture at every turn.

Judaism may often appear ethnocentric, but it has developed a multitude of institutions to preserve its ambiguity and diversity. Foremost among these is the cultural tradition of argument itself.

Sigmund Freud believed that this resistance to authority has primordial roots. According to Freud, the first Jews actually murdered Moses for his burdensome strictures and then buried the memory, passing down the trauma of the experience from generation to generation. He saw this trauma manifested in the relationship of Jews to authority and in their violence toward their own most moral leaders. Freud believed the Jews fixated on the murder of their first spiritual leader but buried the memory, excising it from scriptures and creating through oral tradition a second good Moses, whom they might revere. But according to Freud, the suppressed memory resurfaces periodically in attacks on their leaders.[91]

While he backs up this otherwise bizarre argument with extraordinary textual evidence, little of it has matched up with the later findings of Biblical scholars. Like much in Freud, the retelling is best interpreted as mythological. What he is pointing to is the tortured relationship of Jews to authority and the tendency of Jews to martyr their prophets. We can see this with Jesus, with Spinoza, and with Chomsky today. *Jews educate to argue and debate, then outcaste those Jews who challenge the rigid codes they have learned to debate, only to later make of them heroes.* In this way, the remnant of Jews now challenging the abuses of Israel may later prove to be its prophets.

If Israel fails morally it will fail institutionally. If it fails institutionally it will be because it did not include that part of its tradition that is now raging against its hard heartedness, thrashing against its injustice, and throwing its heart at the wicked rigidity of an increasingly militarized state. The cadence of my language and the moral force which lies behind it mirrors that of a longstanding prophetic tradition. It is an ancient tale that lies at the core of the Jewish tradition. The nature of the tradition and the long history of casting out its own prophetic voices suggests that Jews should not be so quick to condemn opponents of the occupation. For it may be the case that future generations will look upon these fallen prophets as the true bearers of the Jewish tradition – especially if the state of Israel ultimately fails.

Freud's theory may not have withstood the test of archeological and historiographical research, but he saw all of this coming with the foresight of a prophet. Even as the Third Reich grew in power through the thirties, both Freud and Einstein, as well as the more esoteric Martin Buber and Gershom Scholem, opposed the effort to build an exclusively Jewish state in Palestine. While each of them had their own views on the matter, their general concern lay in the inevitable injustices Jews would inflict on the native Palestinians. It was a structural defect that no amount of argument could wash away.

As is the case with most human passions, Freud saw the effort in pathological terms. It appeared to him an effort to instill in Jews a mass consciousness, complete with its own imagined national identity. This he thought could only end in ruin, both for the native Palestinians, who would be made second class citizens in any future Jewish state, and for the Jews themselves, who would be reduced to a mass where previously they were individuals. It is perhaps for this reason he split the founding father of Judaism into two. Moses became both the authoritarian murdered by his own people and another kinder and more inclusive leader. As Jacqueline Rose notes, in a brilliant exploration of the inner life of Israel, right at the moment Jews were most in need of unity, Freud refused to provide it, opting instead for ambiguity and the ability to walk between worlds.[92]

More than ever, the Jews of Israel need to learn again to walk between worlds. And the Jews of the diaspora need to remind them how it is done.

Many of the Jews most likely to challenge the abuses of Israel are secular, or else their hearts are tied to other more esoteric traditions. Many have come to feel alienated from Judaism and see no use for it in a world of increasing diversity. Many simply want no part in some group that would seek to limit their sense of self to something so shallow as their ethnicity.[93] And because of this, it has become easy for them to be marginalized and treated as "self hating Jews." Ironically, it is just these Jews who might be most needed to sustain the dialectic that has long made Judaism thrive. It is their moral and prophetic challenge that might make Judaism last. And it is their unwillingness to be a part of any religion that would only have people like themselves as members that might push Judaism once again to reinvent its traditions and adapt itself to a new age.

Judaism is less threatened by the anti-Semites on the outside than those on the inside. Jews who would equate their religion with a state, and their identity with its actions, build for themselves a house on sand. They degrade their religion to the compromises and corruptions inherent to all states. And they cramp the Jewish identity into so tight a box it will squeeze out its most brilliant and innovative thinkers. It is time to reclaim the secularity, the diversity, the ambiguity, and the cosmopolitanism of Judaism. It is time to imagine a future in which Jews build bridges between worlds instead of destroying infrastructure, in which the tradition of argument is deepened so as to include the other, and ultimately the world.

PART IV

THE DOGS THAT DO NOT
BARK IN PALESTINE

THE DOGS THAT DO NOT
BARK IN PALESTINE

A classic Sherlock Holmes story tells of a winning race horse that is taken in the night and its owner killed. In his investigation, Holmes draws attention to "the curious incident of the dog in the night-time." But his interlocutor interjects, "the dog did nothing in the night-time." To which Holmes replies, "that was the curious incident." *Sometimes it is the dogs who do not bark that are the real story.*[94]

When the watchdog press repeatedly fails to bark on a major issue, we would do well to ask why. The conservative Israeli Sharon administration releases a report stating a third of all settlement lands have been stolen from private Palestinian deed holders. UNICEF releases a report condemning Israel for kidnapping Palestinian children in the night and beating them in an effort to turn them into informers. Human Rights Watch releases a report stating Hamas is not actually using human shields and thus the Israeli bombardment of dozens of schools and hospitals in Gaza is not only ethically controversial but gratuitous. And all the while, the watchdog press is silent.

It is enough to make one ask what tail is wagging these quiet dogs. But while supporters of Israel are well positioned to censor the truth about the occupation, and while many journalists, including myself, have tales to tell of their work on Israel being suppressed, it may be the case that the dogs have simply had their attention diverted. The language through which Israel's actions are framed may be the real story of the dogs who didn't bark.

Language shapes experience, it directs our attention, and tells us what is important. According to the cognitive scientist, George

Lakoff, our ideas of the world are built up through cognitive frames. Frames shape perception through subtle metaphors concerning the way the world is ordered. When development is conceived of through the metaphor *higher*, and *higher* is equated with *better*, this is not an ethical argument but rather a set of frames. It allows a person to jump from the argument that something is *more developed* to the argument that it is *more moral* without actually making a moral argument.[95]

This is dangerous because more developed nations are not always more moral. But this is precisely what supporters of Israel suggest, forgetting their own tragic history with a pathologically developed Germany. There are other frames shaping our perceptions on this issue we would all do well to acknowledge. News sources tend to speak of a Middle East "conflict." But the word "conflict" is a frame that has several consequences for how we conceive of the situation. There must be at least two sides to every conflict. But if there are two sides, then each side deserves to be heard and each side must take responsibility for perpetuating the conflict. Where there is conflict, fair minded people listen and tell both sides, because when both sides are heard conflicts can be resolved and this leads to peace. But the occupation of Palestinian Territories is arguably more like a case of *theft.*

Israeli courts have long recognized it to be an occupation, and the occupation involves the theft of Palestinian groundwater[96] and the theft of privately owned Palestinian land,[97] which is being colonized with Israeli settlements. While thefts also involve conflicts we do not tend to frame them as such. For doing so puts the thief on an equal footing with his victim. And this fails to capture the essence of what is important about theft.

What is important in a case of theft is not peace but rather restitution. If the family of a thief were to begin speaking of the "conflict" with his victim, we would recognize at once that something is amiss, that our perception of the situation is being manipulated. Framing thefts as conflicts makes them more likely to occur in the future, and this can only benefit the thieves.

Similarly, the occupation is inherently abusive, as military occupations tend to be. Among other things, it involves arresting children, killing protesters, and searching civilians at check points, as
most occupations do. While cases of abuse are also conflicts, we do
not tend to frame them as such. For framing abuse as conflict favors
the abuser.

A woman may struggle against her rapist but we do not tend
to call this conflict. The Solidarity movement may have struggled
against the Soviet Union in 1989, but we did not tend to call it a
conflict for good reason. Not only were the two sides not equal, one
side was struggling against an oppressor. To have framed it as a case
of conflict would have suggested a sort of moral equality between
the two sides and this would have been inappropriate.

There is a conflict between Israelis and Palestinians, but it is a
conflict that is perpetuated not through a failure to understand the
other side but rather through theft and abuse. The failure to highlight
this abuse distorts the nature of the relationship in the minds of onlookers. Supporters of Israel often demand "balance" in discussing
the issue but this is also a metaphor, which suggests two sides that
need to be weighed equally, where giving equal weight is a sort of
justice. But giving equal weight to the arguments of an abuser is
just the opposite of justice, for it allows them to set the terms of the
debate, which will always be set in their own favor.

Giving equal weight to lies simply means drifting further from
the truth. And there are not two sides to be heard but rather many.
Hearing them all is not balance but comprehensiveness, and comprehensiveness requires deeper understanding. But what is essential
is often just the thing that one side does not want us to see. Hence,
attaining understanding and thus comprehensiveness often requires
that one side of the story be comprehended. Otherwise, we will
come to misunderstand what is really happening, and that is neither
just nor good but rather ignorant.

Confucius was once asked what he would do if he were to rule
China. He answered that he would begin by calling things by their
true names.[98] When things are called by their true names, the dogs

will bark when criminals approach. But up to now, our attention has been largely diverted. It is time we take it upon ourselves to frame Israel—to catch it in the act by naming its actions more accurately. We need to catch them at the scene of the crime and call their crimes by their true names.

THE OTHER SIDE OF JERUSALEM

A Palestinian resident of East Jerusalem once took me to his roof-top terrace to explain how Israel is re-conquering the Old City. Whereas Israelis can repair their homes and add structures to their roofs, Palestinian are forbidden from making such improvements, so their homes are left smaller and more dilapidated. Wealthy Jewish groups buy up ancient rooftop crescents to erase the Muslim presence from the city. And the harassment of Palestinian residents and the tensions it creates makes most tourists wary of visiting their quarter.

The effect is that visitors are left with the impression that the mostly Muslim Old City is primarily Jewish, but that is mostly just window dressing. The presumed object of these policies is to cleanse the city of its native Palestinian inhabitants by making them feel the brunt of their second-class citizenship. The declining value of their property makes them all the more ready to leave.

Israel makes life hard for the residents of East Jerusalem in order to nudge them out of the country, but when Palestinians visit family abroad or leave for school, they are sometimes simply forbidden from returning.[99] Palestinian homes are routinely bull-dozed as a punishment for their children running afoul of the state. According to the Israeli Committee Against House Demolitions, 46,000 Palestinian homes have been demolished since 1967.[100] They are often just removed outright to make way for settlers.

As Israeli settlers push their way into Palestinian East Jerusalem, they alter the demographics and culture of the city. Over the past several decades, a few hundred thousand Israeli settlers have built their homes in East Jerusalem, bringing with them a massive police presence, which can leave Palestinians feeling like strangers in their own land.

But Palestinians living in East Jerusalem have it easy compared with those in the West Bank. Passing from East Jerusalem into the West Bank can feel a lot like entering a maximum security prison. The passage through the wall surrounding the West Bank is a gauntlet of security checks, carried out by callous guards who treat the locals like livestock. And the road to the West Bank capital of Ramallah is a depressing scene of ramshackle buildings and poverty.

The wall was built about a decade ago with the express purpose of keeping Palestinian terrorists out. But a Palestinian friend told me both his brothers regularly cross into Israel illegally to find work. And the wall snakes deep into Palestinian territory, splitting farmers from their land and villagers from one another, thus making its construction a massive land grab, which the International Criminal Court has deemed illegal.[101]

The Palestinian West Bank has been under military occupation for half a century now. It was originally acquired in 1967, along with the Syrian Golan Heights and the Egyptian Sinai Peninsula and Gaza Strip. Israel coveted the West Bank for its centrality to Jewish identity, and Jerusalem has remained its crown jewel. Yet, the West Bank was already populated by millions of Palestinians, and Jerusalem was their center of cultural and economic life and the main artery linking their major cities. Hence, the Israeli effort to claim it for their own has been fought street-by-street, with the primary weapons being bulldozers, zoning laws, administrative decrees, and eminent domain.

Over the past several decades Israel has brought close to 750,000 settlers into both the West Bank and East Jerusalem. The settlements have been built strategically so as to break East Jerusalem away from the rest of the West Bank and make forging a viable Palestinian state all but impossible.[102] Hence, when Israel declares their capital to be Jerusalem, it is simply the crowning conception to its long standing colonization.

Israeli settlements are built outside the state of Israel in its occupied territories, thus making the term "settlement" a euphemism for what are actually colonies. Israeli colonists are well-armed and often shoot to kill, thereby immiserating the Palestinians who must live in their near vicinity. The conflicts that naturally arise between colonized Palestinians and Israeli colonists require constant military interventions in which the Israeli military is strongly biased in favor of their own co-religionists and compatriots.

Israeli soldiers are centered at dozens of permanent checkpoints on the main roads, and innumerable "flying" checkpoints that come and go. The checkpoints slow movement and impede economic activity. They allow Israeli Defense Forces to collectively punish whole villages when some of their members protest, and they create a pretext for blackmailing residents to spy on their neighbors. They are the nerve centers of a vast security apparatus and a demeaning source of constant tension, which would be largely unnecessary if not for the settler presence.[103]

Israeli settlements sit high in the hills above most Palestinian villages. Each of them is surrounded by a large ring of cleared land and they are built like fortresses, with their windows facing outward to keep watch over the locals.[104] Israel has destroyed over a million Palestinian olive trees,[105] many of which are ancient, in the effort to punish Palestinians and protect settlers. And clearing their land has often required them to terrorize local residents.

A man in Hebron explained to me how settlers beat his pregnant wife, leading her to miscarry – and then did the same thing when she got pregnant again. Another farmer whose land sat between several settlements that were trying to link themselves together showed me the caves where he and his family were forced to live, because the government had decreed he could build no structures on his land. He reported that he was forbidden from digging wells, as are many Palestinian West Bank farmers, and even from collecting rainwater. In so doing, the government was nudging him off his land but also helping recharge the aquifer from which Israel draws most of its drinking water.

About a third of settlements are built on land stolen from private Palestinian deed holders, according to a study commissioned by the conservative government of Ariel Sharon in 2003.[106] First the state of Israel occupied the land, ruling by a series of military decrees. The settlers then stole the choicest pieces for themselves. Hence, the state was pulled deeper into the West Bank in an effort to protect its citizens. Now, the state is the victim of its own success.

Most people working to end the occupation no longer believe a two-state solution is possible. Activists traveling to the West Bank almost universally report that the built infrastructure and state support for settlers is too great to ever allow for their removal. Their views are formed from on-the-ground experience but they can often seem unimaginative. However, political leaders like former Secretary of State John Kerry, who worked for years to bring the two sides together, have begun to share their pessimism, concluding that continued settlement building makes the prospect of a two-state solution dim.

But if this is the case, then Trump's recent recognition of Jerusalem as the capital of Israel is an unwitting recognition of Israel as an apartheid state. For if his recognition of Jerusalem further entrenches Israel in Palestinian territory, making a two-state solution more difficult to achieve than what top negotiators like Kerry already found next to impossible, then Israel needs to start thinking of West Bank Palestinians as its own.

But if West Bank Palestinians are to be governed by Israel, then Israel will need to face up to the fact that it is now an apartheid state, with two sets of citizens enjoying radically different rights and freedoms, governed by two radically different sets of laws. And the last time the world confronted an apartheid state, it was boycotted and sanctioned until it accepted racial equality. From the moment Israel took the West Bank in 1967, Israeli elders like their first Prime Minister David Ben Grunion have warned that holding onto it would be their undoing. Israelis would do well to remember that the end of apartheid was one of the great achievements of the late-twentieth century, which is justly celebrated the world over. If Israel continues on the path of apartheid, they should prepare to encounter a similar fate.

PROTEST WITH PALESTINIANS

It was the eve of the 2014 attack on Gaza and tensions were heating up in the mixed ethnic neighborhood of Jaffa in South Tel-Aviv. So perhaps it was not the safest time to attend my first pro-Palestinian demonstration, but it was certainly revealing. The most striking thing about it was that the Palestinian protesters appeared so free. It was as if in seeking freedom from Israeli discrimination they had eliminated much of their own.

African-American activists often appear to be liberated through their activism in much the same way, but so much activism among more privileged groups in the United States self-selects for a general sense of discontent. It often seems as if the grumpiest people among them make the biggest show. And the stakes are rarely great enough to touch these protesters in such a personal way as the discrimination experienced by Palestinians and African-Americans, so the issues being protested often feel more abstract. The Palestinian-Israeli activists with whom I spoke in Tel Aviv appeared to define themselves through their activism, though.

There is widespread discrimination against Palestinians not just in the West Bank and Gaza but also within Israel proper – where according to the Adalah legal center there are over 50 laws discriminating against Arabs – but much of it goes unacknowledged and unknown.[107] Consider education. Palestinians are educated under a special curriculum in almost wholly segregated schools.[108] Arab schools tend to be provided about a fifth the funding of Jewish schools,[109] and while Arab students can enter Jewish schools, doing so means enduring significant Zionist indoctrination.[110] It has been related to me that even in the Palestinian schools most Palestinian literature has been barred as political and school principles must be approved by the Israeli secret police.

As it goes for education, so goes it for housing. According to a law passed in 2011, Palestinians can be legally prevented from living on 43 percent of the land in Israel by communities who choose to reject their applications.[111] But it is commonly stated by otherwise reasonable sources that they are not allowed to live on 93 percent of the land, which is technically owned by either the state or para-state organizations, founded prior to the state of Israel.[112] The places they can live have also been prevented from expanding. And yet, the Palestinian population of Israel has grown almost ten-fold since the founding of the state. Palestinians are often prevented from expanding or even renovating their homes, in a part of the world where it is not uncommon to live in ancient buildings. And it is common practice for the state to bulldoze their homes when they are expanded.[113]

The system is unbelievably complex and confusing and the complexity is not neutral. For it serves the purpose of obscuring this discrimination from Israelis, most of whom think Palestinians are fully integrated into their society. After all, they can run for office, eat in the same restaurants, and bathe on the same beaches. But it also gives critics pause; there is always a danger some complexity in the code has been misunderstood and the misunderstanding will be used to demonstrate you do not know what you are talking about. But when it comes to Israeli discrimination against Palestinians within the state, almost every Israeli errs on the side of not knowing enough.

The West Bank may exist in a state of apartheid, but Israel proper is not an apartheid state.

And this brings us back to the protest. It was a mixed ethnic crowd, mostly Palestinian but also perhaps 15 percent Jews, who appeared widely welcomed and integrated into the gathering. There were a lot of wide eyes, broad smiles, big hugs, and little sign of religion. According to one veteran protester, the gathering represented a broad swathe of the Palestinian population in the area, so it was not just some gathering of young people or elites. And the police presence was slight, apparently there to prevent escalations more than to provoke them.

Someone tried to drown out the protest chants by playing loud nationalistic dance music and this was largely ignored. One man jumped out of his car, looking angry and waving an Israeli flag, but he was gently ushered away by the police. I asked the veteran protester if the behavior of the police, which seemed quite calm and professional, was normal and he noted that they were mostly there to contain the protests. And yet, somehow this calm and professional police force had shot this same blond-haired, blue-eyed, Israeli Jewish man in the eye in a peaceful protest when was just 17-years old. I pointed out the contradiction and might have added what he told me later: this very mellow demonstrator, who claimed never to have protested violently, had been arrested for his protesting on 40 separate occasions.

And this is the paradox of the Israeli state. It is so easy to see its civilized side if that is what you want to see. And yet, its brutality is so shielded from view for most supporters of Israel, including the Israelis themselves—until it breaks out in war. It is in a sense the perfect crime in which the criminal covers his tracks so thoroughly that he somehow manages to convince even himself that the crime has not been committed. And yet, one of the lessons of the protest for me was that a broad based, Gandhian non-violent movement, in which protesters were not merely non-violent in their actions but also in their demeanors, might be possible.

There is a long and extensive history of Palestinian use of non-violent tactics like strikes, boycotts and simple protests, which often goes ignored, most notably in the earlier stages of their 1936 uprising against the British and in the First Intifada.[114] But I believe what I am suggesting runs a bit deeper than what has come before. In the same way the Palestinians with whom I was protesting appeared to have thrown off their internal oppression through protest, Jews and Palestinians might through working together in such a movement set in motion a process of reconciliation, which would need to occur for any political resolution to the occupation to succeed. This would be similar to the reconciliation between blacks and whites that occurred in South Africa through work in the African National Congress and became the basis for a much deeper social reconciliation.

Deep, non-violent protest holds the promise of creating space for a wider swathe of the population to join the movement. It is more likely to win friends from the Israeli opposition, it can draw out greater international support, it brings more level-headed leaders to power, it links them more closely to those working on the ground, and it is far more likely to result in the emergence of a democratic state, or states as it may be. It would do wonders for the reconciliation that would make any such a state far more secure and stable and, in the end, viable and sustainable. And it is just such a pleasure to participate in friendly and open hearted work for justice.

WHY NONVIOLENT
MOVEMENTS SUCCEED

Pro-Palestinian activists often say no people in history has ever successfully thrown off an occupation without the use of violence, but the results of a recent study on the effectiveness of nonviolent and violent resistance movements demonstrates just the opposite. Erica Chenowith, of the University of Denver, studied every major resistance movement going back to 1900 and found that violent movements achieved their goals only 26 percent of the time, whereas nonviolent movements did so 53 percent of the time – making the nonviolent movements about twice as effective. And they have been becoming ever more effective over time.[115]

She notes that a commitment to nonviolence enhances a campaign's domestic and international legitimacy. And it encourages more broad based participation, which translates into greater pressure being placed on the regime. Attacks on violent movements are also easier to justify, whereas attacks on nonviolent movements are more likely to backfire. Similarly, members of the public tend to perceive violent movements as having maximalist goals, whereas they perceive nonviolent movements as being more moderate in their aims.

When most people think of nonviolent resistance, they tend to think of mass demonstrations, yet nonviolent resistance involves a whole toolkit of strategies and tactics. You can boycott, divest and sanction, of course. But you can also hold sit-ins and die-ins. You can creatively name and shame the perpetrators of oppression. You can stand on the rooftops at night and beat on pots and pans. And you can use satire and humor to draw out the absurd claims of those in power.[116]

The creativity employed in nonviolent resistance campaigns is sometimes ingenious. Just before Serbian protesters overthrew Slobodan Milosevic in 1999, they set up garbage cans in public parks to which they attached his photo and a baseball bat. Anyone who wished could drop in a small coin and then beat on his image. Not having a law under which they might prosecute the garbage can beaters, the episode ended when the police arrested the garbage cans themselves to the delight of demonstrators.

This sort of creativity can galvanize the attention of the press while protecting protesters from violence. In another instance Serbian protesters knew they needed to demonstrate how brutal the regime could be, but they did not want to get people needlessly hurt. So they sent protesters down a street where they knew the police would attack, and they put young women in the front so they could get a picture of the abuse. But right when the police launched into beating them, they took their photos, and then each woman was surrounded by several men who spirited them to the back of the line, after which the biggest and burliest men went to the front lines to take a beating.

Nonviolent resistance can be academic, diplomatic, and philosophical. It can be artistic, musical and dramatic. And in its most well-known form, it can be ethical and spiritual. The various means through which nonviolent resistance is expressed can foster development in both the human spirit and culture alike. Many supporters of violent Palestinian resistance claim it gives the people dignity, and this may be true. But the dignity provided to the small percentage of the population that participates in violent resistance may pale in comparison to the flourishing of the human spirit afforded through nonviolent resistance.

Perhaps one of the most overlooked forms of resistance is the simple use of reason on social media. Through debating with opponents, Palestinians, Turks and Iranians of all ages can offer up an endless resistance through which they might grow and develop in intelligence, patience, and the ability to think clearly. And they can garner the support of other thinkers the world over.

Nonviolent resistance also develops civil society for it challenges people to come together in new and creative ways. Since much nonviolent resistance is creative, expressive, and intellectual, it challenges people to organize themselves around human expression. This means that nonviolent organizers will tend to focus on inclusion of differences, both within and without the group. Nonviolent movements are usually safer, but even when they are not, they tend to be possessed of a calm that can be more inviting to women and the old. For this reason, Chenoweth found that nonviolent movements were usually about four times as large as violent movements.

The kind of well-developed civil society that nonviolent movements contribute to can also serve as the foundation for a healthy democracy. Upon attaining power, resistance movements will bring their own leaders to power. Violent movements tend to bring to power authoritarians, like Fidel Castro and Mao Zedong, while nonviolent movements tend to bring to power leaders who possess the flexibility of mind necessary for democracy to flourish, like India's Nehru and Czechoslovakia's Vaclav Havel. Nonviolent leaders are more likely to rely on persuasion and reason, for they are only able to rise to power insofar as they can convince people of the rightness of their cause. Thus, how a people resists will often determine the nature of the government they get when they come to power.

Palestinians have a right to resist the occupation violently, as does any people living under occupation – especially when it has been going on for decades And it is up to themselves to choose their own means of resistance. But the sort of traumas inflicted by the occupation and other forms of oppression will tend to make violent resistance a mesmerizing option. Once it starts it is hard to stop. And the forceful power of violence can sometimes make it seem like the only game in town. This can easily suck them into endless cycles of violence, which bring to their leadership the most hard-hearted and authoritarian members of their society, just the people who are least likely to win a state or citizenship in a shared state.

The strength of violent resistance is largely an illusion, because it invites such strong counter-resistance; because so few can participate; because it turns off passive supporters; because it brings all the wrong people to power; and because it is so closed to creative possibilities. Violence clouds the mind with rigid fixations, and it makes everything more difficult to organize. But if all this is not reason enough for Palestinians to adopt a nonviolent strategy, perhaps the fact that the Israelis possess all the weapons and are willing to use them is reason enough.

HOW JESUS UNDERMINED
THE ROMANS

What do you call a Christian who opposes the occupation of Palestine by undermining its socio-economic and religious under-pinnings? Among other things, you might call him Christ.

There is a quiet sea change in support for Israel among American Christians.[117] This transformation is so powerful it might ultimately end the occupation of Palestine by shifting support away from Israel, but it has largely gone ignored. Conservative evangelical Christians, who have been a bastion of support for Israel, are increasingly scrutinizing the state's human rights abuses. Key leaders are dropping their support, while the younger generation opposes as much as it supports Israel.

Meanwhile, more liberal Mainline Protestant churches, like the Methodists, Lutherans, and United Church of Christ, are seriously debating divestment from Israel.[118] Mainline Protestants are core to American society and were crucial to the Anti-Slavery and Civil Rights movements. They fought and eventually overcame the Jim Crow system of racial injustices upon which South Africa modeled their own system of Apartheid. And their increasing support for Palestinian human rights could ultimately turn the tide in favor of Palestinians.

It is a great irony that American Christians often support the occupying Israel over the occupied Palestinians. Jesus lived and died in occupied Palestine, after all. And he was crucified at the hands of the occupying Romans. His mission was in many ways a response to the suffering engendered through occupation.[119] And a substantial portion of the Palestinian population is Christian, the most well integrated in the Arab world. Jesus spends most of the Gospels comforting the marginalized, criticizing the wealthy, and preaching love. But the occupation is ever-present in the tensions with Rome, the constraints placed on the Jewish religious establishment, and most of all in his own persecution.

Biblical scholarship has in recent decades revealed a more nuanced picture of the socio-economic conditions of Israel under Roman occupation. The Biblical scholar, John Crossan, notes the people whom Jesus saved were often suffering from disease and impoverishment because the Roman occupation was milking their land of resources. And like many who suffer from such poverty and social marginalization, they probably had high levels of mental illness and were ready for a savior, thus making early Christianity in many ways a response to occupation.[120] Most Biblical scholars consider substantial portions of the Gospels to be fiction, but what matters is the Jesus Christians have come to emulate.

Christians have been primed to support Israel. According to Biblical legend, when Moses led the Jews out of Egypt, God commanded them to commit genocide no less than five times. God repeatedly told them to kill every man, woman, child, and living thing as they conquered the Canaanites, Amalekites, and Philistines. Recent archeological digs have turned up little, if any, evidence of these massacres or, more generally, the exodus legend itself. Most historians and archeologists have come to believe instead that the Jews were indigenous to what is now Israel and Palestine.[121] But three millennia later, the early Zionists reenacted the exodus myth when they took these lands by force. Fleeing from oppression, they once again ethnically cleansed native Palestinians and proclaimed their victory an act of God.

The Biblical mythos that underlay the Israeli national narrative of reclaiming the Promised Land probably accounts for a substantial portion of Christian support for Israel. But it is a narrative founded on a series of falsehoods that are increasingly being exposed. Israel was advertised as "a land without a people for a people without a land," but the early Zionists took over existing and often ancient cities.[122] They did not "make the desert bloom," as is so often claimed, but rather took over lands that had been in continual agricultural production for thousands of years, irrigated with waters taken from occupied Palestinian territories.

Jews at the time of Christ struggled to formulate an effective response to the Roman occupation. The Zealots fought it, the Essenes sought to escape it, and the Pharisees collaborated in the interest of religious self-preservation. But Jesus was different: he did not resist the Roman occupation of Palestine, he undermined it. He undermined the occupation by placing God above the occupying power and by using love to abolish the distinction between occupier and occupied. He undermined it by challenging religious authorities that were accommodating the occupation and by presenting an alternative vision so compelling it would eventually win over the occupiers. While Jesus was crucified by the occupying power, the Romans ultimately adopted Christianity as their state religion. Jesus' response to the occupation was unique and hard to replicate. And it is important to recognize that if Biblical scholars agree on anything about Jesus it is that he was a Jew.[123] But it is a model that might inspire Christian support for Palestinians, and this support may be crucial to ending the occupation.

Jesus represents a sort of middle way between violent resistance, passive acquiescence, and collaboration. There is no one-state or two-state solution in the teachings of Jesus. He challenges worldly powers without giving worldly solutions. He protests Roman rule through humility. The Biblical scholar Marcus Borg points out that he entered Jerusalem on the back of a donkey, for instance, on the same day as the annual Roman celebration of their power.[124] Jesus often appears in the Gospels as a sort of anarchist, who places his faith in a higher principle of order than any humans might create, and it is just this faith that "might move mountains." Jesus opens the way to a transformation of the heart that might ultimately bring down inner and outer walls alike. But he challenges power at every turn. Oppressed from within and from without, in a culture prone to implosion, it is a model Palestinians would do well to consider.

Meanwhile, a more historically grounded notion of Jesus challenges Christians to step out of their comfort zones and seek a higher and more just order of human affairs. It challenges anti-occupation activists to look for a wider range of forces that might ultimately erode Israeli power. And it challenges global powers to reconsider the nature of power itself. Like most scriptures, the Gospels give no definite response to power. But a more historically grounded exploration of the life of Jesus reveals a powerful if unusual Palestinian ally, sacrificing himself in an epic confrontation with occupying power and occupied collaborators alike—and ultimately winning.

Christians have been seduced by an Old Testament view of Israel profoundly at odds with the New Testament. Whereas the God of the Torah is a tribal God of vengeance, the Christian God is a God of love. It is a universal God, who commands forgiveness and is free of tribal affiliations. Judaism may be a progressive religion that has long evolved past its founding scriptures, but these scriptures can be used to both inspire and justify the occupation of Palestine. A focus on the real Jesus and his response to the occupation reframes everything. Palestinians have a friend in Jesus and we would all do well to make use of his unusually powerful connections.

THE DECLINE AND FALL
OF THE ISRAELI OCCUPATION

A time will come when the foundations sustaining every brutal regime suddenly start to crumble.

Few notice when the cracks first appear, but then they grow larger and suddenly everything starts to seem possible. This is the way it was with the fall of the Berlin Wall, and with it the Soviet Empire. And for a brief historical moment it seemed to be the case with the Arab Spring.

It felt much the same, as the coalition sustaining American support for Israel for almost three generations began to crumble before our eyes in the spring following the attack on Gaza.

The activist organizer, Peter Cohen, recently suggested that the crack in Jewish-American opinion is the shot that will blow up the Death Star. Israel has long been dependent on bi-partisan support, and much of this has been Jewish, but American Jews are increasingly divided on Israel. And liberals in general are fast turning against the Jewish state. Suddenly, things that had just seemed beyond contemplation were being spoken about openly by members of an American Presidential administration. The American nuclear deal with Iran would bring a fundamental geo-political realignment in the Middle East—and with it, the America-Israel alliance would likely be downgraded. The ground was shifting under our feet as new vistas opened on the horizon.

When American issues become partisan, taking a stance for your own side in the liberal-conservative divide becomes a matter of identity. Liberals and conservatives throw everything they have got at each other, mobilizing television and radio networks, activist organizations, pundits, and lobbies. The fact that the American political system is largely plutocratic and controlled by the wealthy may actually make the fighting more intense. The payoff of all this criticism does not lie so much in the passage of legislation, which usually requires compromise, but rather the self-definition of American culture. American political fights are largely about who we are as a people and these sorts of fights can be intensely moral.

It is a serious infringement of national sovereignty when a foreign leader speaks before the legislature of a major power in order to undermine the foreign policy agenda of its President.

But it is a far more serious offense when the foreign leader has just conducted espionage against the President and passed confidential state information to the Republican opposition, as the Obama administration says Netanyahu did. If they are right, Republican leaders complicit in this coordinated attack cannot be tried for treason, but their patriotism can be drawn into question.

Meanwhile, the Netanyahu administration, whose leadership of Israel was just reconfirmed, can expect a backlash from American liberals. Now the Obama administration is talking about recognizing a Palestinian state through a once controversial U.N. resolution. They have just made Israel's secret nuclear program public, which has never yet been declared. And they are saying any moves to annex portions of the West Bank might undermine the America-Israel alliance.

What might be next?

Since expressing criticism of Israel has come at a heavy price for American politicians and members of the media for generations, Americans know little if anything about Israel's repeated abuses of international law and the Palestinian people. Few know that a third of the land on which Israel's settlements are built was stolen from private Palestinian deed holders[125] or that since the occupation began Israel has destroyed over a million West Bank olive trees.[126] Few know that Israel steals 80-90 percent of West Bank groundwater and makes building new wells virtually illegal.[127] Few know Israel arrests Palestinian children in the night and tries to coerce them into becoming informants or that, according to U.N. figures, they killed 245 Gazan civilians for every Israeli civilian killed in the last war.[128]

When the fighting on this issue starts up, Americans are in for a shock.

Regimes can fall unexpectedly when a state's debt becomes so great it can no longer afford to maintain its imperial domain, as Americans are fast realizing in regards to much of the American empire. They can fall when demographic changes bring about new political alignments, as is currently occurring within Israel. They can fall when a generation of leaders that once controlled everything dies off, as is happening with many of the key leaders in America's Israel lobby. And they can fall when ideologies become outworn, as is happening with Zionism for American Jews.

These sorts of changes are like the shifts in deep oceanic currents. We do not know what has hit us until we find ourselves far off course. And they are all transforming America's relationship to Israel. There is a massive geopolitical realignment happening in the Middle East and Israel is panicking. The nuclear deal with Iran is a part of this realignment, as is the implosion of Syria and the banding together of Iraqi Shia, who are supported by Iran. But America's geopolitical shift toward East and Southeast Asia is also important. Both the George W. Bush and the Obama administrations attempted a "pivot toward Asia," a massive geopolitical shift in attention that seeks to contain a rising China. But this shift is being prevented by Israel, which continually draws America into the Middle East.

Meanwhile, the crack in bi-partisan support for Israel is so unusually powerful because Israel is so shockingly awful that when Democrats want to beat Republicans over the head with dead Palestinian babies, there will be no shortage. When they want to put Republicans in a box, they will have a constant string of facts and metaphors with which to keep them occupied. And American's jaws will drop over what they learn. If this process continues, longtime critics of the occupation can expect to find themselves out of work as more mainstream groups take over their job of criticizing Israel.

THE POLITICS OF
PALESTINIAN POSSIBILITY

The landscape of the Middle East may have been fundamentally transformed when Israeli Prime Minister, Benjamin Netanyahu, renounced
the possibility of a Palestinian state and was re-elected.[129] For he tore
off the mask of civility at just the right time for the Obama administration to talk seriously of supporting a U.N. resolution declaring a
Palestinian state. But Netanyahu not only challenged the goals of a
decades-long American-led negotiating process, he also challenged
the Obama administration on its nuclear deal with Iran, one of its sig-
nature achievements. Suddenly, the American political consensus in
favor of supporting Israeli interests seemed to be faltering.

This placed the movement to end the occupation of Palestine
at a crossroads. The two-state solution is increasingly seen as dead,
due to the ever-increasing number of settlers living in the West Bank,
whom activists do not expect the state to be able to remove in the
event of an agreement, and the extent of Israeli built infrastructure,
which has broken up the land and made it difficult to conceive of
the contours of a future Palestinian state. But supporters of a single
democratic state with equal rights for all lack a realistic strategy to
attain it in the near future and have barely articulated their vision to
decision makers.

A single democratic state, with equal rights for all, in Israel and
the occupied Palestinian territories, would provide a home for both
Jews and Palestinians alike. It would declare everyone a human first
and a Palestinian or Jew second. And it would end the contortions
that sustain the idea of an ethno-democratic, Israeli state.[130] But

achieving a single democratic state will involve thinking and debating a whole lot more about what is to come. And it will involve not only selling the "one-state solution" to the world, but of Palestinians as partners in that state as well. World leaders have not yet bought into the idea and even activist supporters struggle to explain how it can be achieved. Nor is the current movement to end the occupation ready to achieve this end.

The members of that movement have been struggling to expose Israeli human rights abuses for years and have succeeded in bringing the plight of the Palestinians to the attention of the world. But if movement members are to ride the waves of this victory to the end of the occupation and the full enfranchisement of Palestinians, the movement itself must pass into a new phase. It is a frustrated movement, many of whose members have been traumatized by a two-generation long occupation and countless wars. This frustration is often emotively expressed and shades into hatred. The hatred is directed at Israel's strongest supporters of the occupation but also its more passive supporters and quiet opposition as well. Sometimes it even targets Jews in general.

There is a tremendous cost to be paid in the expression of these sentiments. It leads liberal American Jews and moderate progressives to mistrust Palestinians. And it keeps the Germans, and with them the European Union, from becoming supporters of the Palestinian cause. Without the support of liberal American Jews and Germans, it will be extremely difficult to pressure Israel without provoking a fight to the finish. The idea that Palestinians can somehow attain the military firepower to defeat Israel once and for all is unrealistic and signals to many that Palestinians are not ready to live in peace. If the movement to end the occupation is to achieve a single democratic state, it needs to change its tone, unequivocally renounce racism against anyone, and begin thinking more strategically. But its members also need to open their hearts to the vision of Arabs and Jews living together in peace and some measure of harmony. Otherwise, there is reason neither for Jews nor the world to embrace the one-state solution.

Enter the Fair Courts Resolution, a visionary proposal that would lay the foundations for the one-state solution. The proposal is the brainchild of Mike Burch, an American publisher of Holocaust and Nakba poetry and a good friend with whom I have worked on the project. Burch envisions a U.N. resolution that would mandate fair and equal courts in areas under Israeli control. Fair courts set up orderly procedures by which the most dangerous members of society are kept watch over. They end the rule of the strong in favor of the rule of law. Fair courts lay down the rules by which all citizens are expected to relate and so set the norms of everyday interactions. This serves as a sort of social grease, which makes these interactions easier. And fair courts institutionalize the principle of moral equality, which is the foundation for equal human and political rights. When the law treats people as equals, they start to see one another as such, which is in many ways the foundation of all civilized society.

The resolution starts with the baby-step of basic civil rights. It could even be initiated through a series of steps, starting with the rights of children. Since it would probably take decades for the Israeli legal system to establish equal civil rights, the resolution would be retractable and would probably involve an ongoing series of political battles, which is just as it should be. For the struggle for equal civil rights and a stake in the system would mark a sea change in the Palestinian struggle in that it would shift the struggle into the courts and into reasoned debate.

The resolution would be enacted by Israeli courts and overseen by a U.N. appointed court with the power to set in motion a series of escalating sanctions should Israel be found noncompliant. It can be scaled up with ever more stringent resolutions. And for the risk-averse, who worry the great is the enemy of the good, it is entirely compatible with a two-state solution. Fair courts would put an end to some of the worst Israeli abuses, like settler youths terrorizing local Palestinians, Israeli Defense Force extremists shooting protesters randomly, and late-night child arrests.[131] Ordinary Israelis and their American defenders often do not know about these abuses, but fair courts would bring them to light.

The time may not be ripe for such a resolution, but it is not hard to foresee a time in which Israel will be so pressured by boycotts and sanctions that it becomes more open to such solutions. Another scenario finds Israel plagued by a Third Intifada, or Palestinian uprising. Yet another imagines the inflow of Jews reversing itself and Israel becoming the victim of rapid demographic decline, as the most educated and capable Jews seek a better life in Europe or America. Any of these situations could bring about a sea change in Israeli public opinion that would make previously impossible visions begin to look like realistic possibilities.

What we are left with today is a bundle of possible goods that might be attained by Palestinians, which have yet to be organized into an immediately realizable political program. These goods range from self-governance to the right-of-return for Palestinians abroad; from access to the sea to the ability to work in the economically more developed state of Israel; from citizenship in Israel, with full civil and political rights, to an end to the siege of Gaza.

Sari Nusseibeh, the former Palestinian mayor of East Jerusalem and a nonviolent leader of the First Intifada, argues in an unusually brilliant book, *What is a Palestinian State Worth?*, that Palestinians should consider more creative ways of dividing up these goods.[132] Nusseibeh notes that much of what Palestinians want may not require a state and that a state will come with its own challenges, which may not prove so easy to surmount. The fate of more recent new states like South Sudan, Eritrea, Bosnia, and Kosovo highlights the troubles Palestinians will confront in building a state from scratch. There is still much interest among Palestinians outside of activist circles in a two-state solution; and there is still little support among Palestinians and Israelis alike for a single democratic state with equal rights for all. Meanwhile, the bundle of goods for which Palestinians are negotiating might be divided up in entirely new and unforeseen combinations.

But a politics of the possible dictates that we must remain open to creative solutions.

Since we do not know what the future will bring, and since

Palestinians must determine their own fates, it is important the movement to end the occupation work positively toward goals that are open-ended. But it would do well to begin talking about solutions, for a movement paralyzed by indirection is a movement that will be hard to trust. It is also important the movement shows a capacity to celebrate victories. This will signal that it knows when to quit, and it will begin drawing to the movement the sort of people who are accustomed to winning. The movement needs to set in motion a snowball effect by which each small win builds momentum for the next bigger win. The movement to end the occupation will need to become much stronger. Members need to breath deep, open up to new supporters, and begin thinking strategically.

PART V

LAUGHING ISIS OFF THE FACE OF THE EARTH

LAUGHING ISIS OFF THE
FACE OF THE EARTH

A friend in Tunisia tells me the unemployed young men sit around and watch Isis videos and porn. A best friend of his even joined up and got killed. Tunisia is the only democracy to be born of the Arab Spring, and the young women there seem educated and liberated. But unemployment and a sense of hopelessness are high among young men and they are joining Isis in droves.

It all makes the pseudo-religious cult look a bit less evil and more like some masturbatory power fantasy. It is time we explore why we are so afraid of a relatively small group of hopeless young men with nothing to lose and learn to see the absurdity in their pretensions. In so doing, we might puncture some of their aura of invincibility and nonviolently combat their propaganda.

But if you want to start by blaming Islamic culture, just remember all those Christian Germans who joined the far more genocidal Nazis not so long ago when they were unemployed and hopeless. Sometimes it seems as if young men will join anything that promises to give them a sense of purpose. However, Isis is not just any movement. Here in the West, they have come to represent a sort of post-apocalyptic return to barbarism.

The vacuum of state failure in Syria and Iraq has become the occasion for the rise of a postmodern nihilism dressed up in religious drag. Isis represents not only everything that could go wrong in human nature and society but also a frightening vision of the future. There is even an Isis video of masked men racing down desert roads shooting up the passengers of random cars, like extras in some Mad Max remake.

Yet, ours is a remarkably peaceful phase of history with fewer wars and fewer people being killed in war than perhaps any time in history, notes Steven Pinker in his rigorously researched, *Better Angels of Our Nature.*[133] Isis reminds us of the cruelties to which humanity is heir. We may shudder at our first glimpse of a beheading, but the guillotine was introduced in France just before the Revolution of 1789 in order to make executions painless.[134] And the Reign of Terror following the Revolution was far more bloody than the Isis hit squads.

We may express shock at the genocide Isis is carrying out against the Yezidis and other minorities, but it was not so long ago that one of the most respected presidents in American history obliterated not just Hiroshima and Nagasaki but also Dresden, Tokyo, and Kyoto. Isis represents not only the barbarities humanity might at any time commit, but the repressed shadow of an America that might still at any moment completely obliterate the world.

Isis provides a glimpse of what might lie beneath the surface of institutional breakdown. The vision frightens us because we know the coming century will be characterized by a multitude of global challenges that might very well stress the institutions of civilization to the breaking point.

Isis seems to present less a glimpse of some lower phase of human development and more a case of developmental collapse. This is what happens when the effort to develop socially and politically implodes and the bottom drops out.

Globalization is now searing through every part of the world. It is liquefying settled ways of life and increasing the burdens of governance. For where customs are no longer clear, the state must step in. But in all too many cases, the state has simply buckled under the strain. As a result, the number of failed states in the world has been growing annually for some time, and groups like Isis and Boko Haram are filling the power vacuum left in their wake.

The specter of runaway global warming may also lurk behind our fears. There are simply too many variables to bear in mind to think about climate change rationally, so our thinking on the matter

drifts into science fiction fantasies of social collapse and desertification. And into the inferno of the imagination slips the self-styled
darkness of Isis, offering up a nightmarish vision of how globalization and environmental collapse might converge to unleash civilization's long suppressed id.

My first book, *Convergence: The Globalization of Mind*, explores the many ways we struggle to think coherently about something so vast as a world. There is a strong tendency when thinking
through so many variables to become overwhelmed. The effort constitutes a developmental leap for which we are all to often unprepared. We shuffle wildly through scenarios of what the world may
become as we are inundated with new perspectives and possibilities.[135] And Isis presents an eerie vision of how everything might fall
apart.

Isis brands our visions of the future with the stamp of nihilistic
hate. But they are not nearly so murderous as the Syrian Assad regime. Assad starves whole cities while torturing tens of thousands of
people to death. Videos of laughing Syrian soldiers, bashing heads
against walls and stomping on dead bodies, are often more grim than
their better known Islamopunk counterparts. But Isis has somehow
managed to make murder cool for a certain demented segment of the
population, and it is here where we can have an effect.

The Ghanaian philosopher, Kwame Anthony Appiah, notes in
his highly original work, *The Honor Code: How Moral Revolutions
Happen*, that moral revolutions happen when customs that were
once regarded as honorable instead become an embarrassment.
While in 1750 British noblemen were expected to duel, by 1850 it
had become an occasion for laughter and derision. While in 1850
Chinese women were expected to bind their feet, by 1950 it was a
source of cultural shame.[136]

My ex-partner, Alia Braley, wrote her Harvard Masters thesis
on how to fight Isis nonviolently.[137] Among numerous strategies, she
recommended breaking the trance of fear through satire. Isis may
represent our worst fears of the future and those fears might one day
become manifest. But the fears are now being manufactured, like

the juvenile videos of bearded morons smashing ancient art. As a former leadership coach, I would advise an army of scarcely 30,000 soldiers, taking on much of the world, to focus on its strengths, and it seems that Isis is most skilled at producing videos that play on our fears. Take these away and they are just another band of losers seeking a sense of purpose, who have gotten far too carried away.

If you can't build a civilization, break its art; if you can't find a wife, rape a village girl – so appears to run their reason. However, Braley suggests something deeper and more uplifting than simply laughing them into oblivion. The people of the region need to claim a better vision of the future and combat brand evil with something more inspiring and uplifting than a half-secure existence under corrupt, secular dictators. If Isis represents some of our own worst fears realized, then perhaps we too should spend some time thinking about how to build the future we truly want.

THE POLITICS OF EVIL

After killing his four sons, the Isis militiamen wagered a deal. They would let him go, but if he did not return from the mountain with more families, they would turn his wife and four daughters into sex-slaves. It was a classic double bind: either way the man would not be able to live with his decision. And it was doubly cruel, because it was meant to not only destroy its actual victims but the man who now held their fates in his hands.

When my friend came across him in the refugee camp, he had lost not only his mind, but all ten members of his family as well. The brutality of the Islamic State is stunning. And it is becoming increasingly common to treat them as a sort of archetype of evil, but what exactly we mean by "evil" is unclear. The expression can be a bit like one of those drawers into which we throw all of our junk. We place the cruel, the shameless, the brutal, and the calculating, and all of them acting in tandem, in that catch-all category. But most of us do not really know what we mean when we use the term evil. Often we call things evil simply as a way of resolving our discomfort. We do not understand how people can do what they do and seek to resolve our disbelief by calling it something to which we know how to respond.

The problem with writing of Isis as evil in this way is that this might be exactly what they want, for they initially acquired most of their financial resources from robbing banks, ransoming hostages and looting minorities, before eventually commandeering several lucrative oil-fields. Their horrifying videos make these things easier to achieve because in being confronted by that classic dilemma of your money or your life, most will forfeit their money and escape with their lives. Hence, the more evil they appear, the faster people run, the more they can loot and the more territory they acquire. Thus, treating them as evil may actually facilitate their work.

But when we say they are evil it seems we are getting at the sense that they take pleasure in their cruelty. Most of us do this in little ways, like when we play jokes on friends and revel in their apprehension. But it seems for most people to call this pleasure evil requires that it break its victims physically or mentally, and this is just what the militiamen were doing with the man faced with the impossible wager.

Now there are also many videos of Israeli soldiers reveling in killing Palestinians. Either they make a joke of it with some crude t-shirt or they prank call Gazans telling them their houses or hotels are about to be bombed. But there is a distance and abstraction to this revelry, and it is easy to get the sense that, were they brought face-to-face with their victims, many of them would quickly change their tune.

Israeli Defense Forces also appear to be deliberately killing civilians, and it increasingly seems they are doing this as a form of collective punishment. Sometimes this appears cold and calculating, sometimes hot-headed and hateful. But the cruelty here seems more a source of weakness than strength, a failure to live up to collective national ethical standards that must somehow be explained away. The evil of Isis, on the other hand, appears more a source of strength, something about which they are bragging. Yet, seeing their evil as a source of strength lends to it a greater aura of power that may play into their hands.

The biggest problem with the category of evil when applied to a genocidal militia is that it is so unrealistic. Killing en masse is hard work. The Rwandan Hutus treated their mass murder as a disciplined vocation. They assembled each morning, organized into teams and goaded one another on in what was essentially a nine-to-five job.[138] Carrying out such work requires its own sort of inverted morality. It is similar to the sort of willpower needed to finish a big desert after a filling meal. Sometimes we must push ourselves to do what is wrong in the same ways we push ourselves to do what is right. Never mind that we are only hurting ourselves and others in the process; we somehow feel compelled to continue. Certainly we should expect that many of the Isis militiamen, far from being shameless and bloodthirsty, actually struggle to complete the killings.

We do not know what lies behind the masks of Isis militiamen. We do not know the looks of pleasure or horror they express when they kill en masse. We do not know how they muster up the energy needed to cut off the heads of victims or how they feel as they wash the blood from their hands. But the more we study the organization and the people who are drawn to it the more we find real human beings having real human responses to the atrocities they are committing. Throwing them into the evil drawer and closing it up does not help us to deal with the threats they pose. On the contrary, it is often a way for us to disengage altogether. Not only does this make for poor strategy, but it dehumanizes the whole discourse. All of us become a little less human when we fail to see the ordinary humanity of the perpetrators of crimes against humanity.

LIFE AFTER GENOCIDE
WITH YEZIDIS

There is always the worry when wandering too far off the beaten path that you might be beaten and robbed, and no one will care because you are not one of them.

Just after telling me that only a few tourists pass this way each year, my Kurdish friend and guide left me at this small border town on the Turkish side of Iraq. Now my life is entrusted to a taxi driver, who does not speak a word of English, who is to pick me up at the café where I wait for a couple of hours, to take me to the airport. But the café is an oasis of rolling Central Asian melodies and cool watery mists. And it is a refuge from the stony streets, where Kurdish youths stop and stare.

We came here to visit the Yezidi refugees, streaming in from northern Iraq. It took a friend of a friend of a friend to reach my new friend Murat, at four degrees of separation, but we might as well have met in an artsy coffee shop in a liberal American college town. He is a photographer from a nearby city, and the camp guards seem not to trust these two long-haired men, with no press credentials and no clear plans. But if you want to understand the fate awaiting the Yezidis, you need to understand where they have come from and where they have landed, and this means you must take the time to feel your way into the crosscurrents into which they have been thrown.

The camp is run by the local Kurdistan Workers Party. The PKK, as they are called, used to be a communist but appear to have mellowed. It was the PKK that cleared a path out of the mountains for many of the Yezidis, who were trapped there and dying of thirst. But many in the camp worry the PKK only saved them so they could enlist the young men to fight against the Assad regime in Syria. The PKK is a progressive force in Kurdish society, which is pressing for the equality of women, and as of 2014, they were making peace with the Turkish government.

The man in charge moves with the graceful fluidity of a liberal and broad minded thinker, and he complains to my Kurdish friend that America still lists the PKK as a terrorist organization, though they do not engage in terrorism these days and are now fighting with America against Isis. He neglects to mention their long history of terror attacks, and it is easy to act as if they never happened at all. Still, he tells us we can enter the camp, saying quite sincerely that he can see we are humanists.

The Yezidis I speak with do not trust any group in the Middle East. They say they have suffered 74 genocides since ancient times. And while it is hard to tell exactly what this means, it is clear they feel persecuted. They remind me of many of my Jewish relatives, who migrated from Iraq to Iran shortly after the First World War. My father said he never really fit in until he came to America. And like my father, the Yezidis say they want to leave the Middle East and come to America. My friend and translator, Sivan, goes so far as to say that Yezidis only trust God, the U.N., and the U.S.. But he says that he only trusts the U.S. After all, the recent intervention of the Obama administration just saved them from genocide.

The Yezidis call themselves a minority of the minority Kurds. The roots of their religion remain somewhat obscure. The religion itself is clearly syncretistic and hints at Zoroastrian origins. It may be the original religion of the Kurds, prior to their conversion to Islam. But the religion took shape under a Sufi order in the twelfth century of the common era.[139] Isis calls them atheists and threatens to kill them if they do not convert. But the Yezidis are a remnant of a remnant, and like many small religious sects of the Middle East,[140] resisting assimilation appears to be part of their cultural DNA. Now they are targeted for genocide.

Sivan and I sit and philosophize with a group of young men about the nature of genocide, the unimportance of religion, and the cycle of a life disrupted. The conversation is discontinuous as some drift off, wondering about family that have been left behind. Traumas like these can narrow the scope of life, and yet it is important when everything has been thrown into question to get some distance and explore the options.

There is something exotic about such a small and ancient sect, but these young men are like the Millennial Generation everywhere. They have the same hair cuts, the same phones, the same education, the same soft manners, and the same addiction to Facebook. Their eyes are bright and their faces smart. Even here in the camp, they seem at home in the world and comfortable with diversity. And yet, they are survivors of a genocide that is just getting underway and their fate hangs as if by a geopolitical thread.

It is possible Iraq will become stable and inclusive. It is possible the civil war in Syria will soon end. It is possible the Yezidis will be sheltered by America, Europe, and Turkey. And it is possible the world will continue to become increasingly democratic, and in another generation, Sivan will find himself living at peace with his former persecutors.

But as for now the world is closing in on him, and it is clear his life just got a lot harder. There will be tough choices ahead over which no one should have to struggle. We can help by understanding who these people are and what they need. Now that America has taken it upon itself to protect the Yezidis, we need to understand the geopolitical context into which they have been thrust. And we need to imagine their lives as if they were our own. It is imperative that we understand them enough to not just save their lives but to allow them to flourish, and this means that after we have absorbed the horror stories of genocide, we need to open up a window into their worlds so they might find a way out.

BECOMING A REFUGEE

Temperatures soared to 105 degrees in the refugee camp, and flies swarmed around my exhausted and dehydrated body. My clothes reeked of sweat upon sweat. Were this to become my home, it was easy to imagine how the stench, the exhaustion, the uncertainty, and the boredom might wear me down. But this was only my first day meeting with the Yezidis. They had just become refugees, and like myself, they were rapidly adjusting to their new circumstances. Over time they might pass from being temporarily located in a refugee camp to being refugees. But this world was still new.

Their lives had been suddenly upended a few weeks ago when they awoke to phone calls in the middle of the night, telling them Isis was coming and they had better run. Some fled to the mountains, where they would later begin dying of hunger and thirst. Some stayed behind, laughing at others for their cowardice, and were almost certainly killed. The ones in this camp had headed for the border where Turkey meets Iraq. Those who had not taken their passports were settled in refugee camps in Iraq, while those who brought their passports crossed over to camps in Turkey. There we would talk for hour-upon-hour about their experiences as they slowly pieced together their fates.

Most had been at the camp for about ten days and most had lost family. One man was the sole survivor of twenty-one family members. He wandered the camp depressed and dejected and would not talk about what happened. Another man told of his wife dying and a child being lost in a crowd. Yet another witnessed the massacre of 110 fellow villagers from the mountains through binoculars. All in all, it sounded like classic tales of genocide. Yet, there were others whose eyes were still bright with hope. One young woman who had lost all of her family beamed with excitement as a crowd of people questioned me as to the prospect of coming to America. Everyone it seemed wanted to come to the land of opportunity of their saviors.

Then there was Jro, a seventeen year old, whose eyes glowed with playful humor. Were he in America, he might have been a high school Romeo. He was the kind of person who brightens up any gathering, and it seemed at times there was no better argument against Isis than his gentle friendliness. His love was a triumph in the face of hate. And there was Ishmael, who sat pensive, his thin cheeks pulled back and his eyes narrowed in thought. He had just graduated from college with a degree in computer technology, and it was clear he was smart. But he had left family behind in Iraq, so while he sat with us all day and spoke passable English, he said little.

Each of them were passing from one life into another. Everyone in the camp had lost something. The young people had lost little of material value and they seemed more easily to let go of their loved ones. But their dreams were being broken just as they were getting started in life. This was the real tragedy of the camp. Their life trajectories were a microcosm of the larger Yezidi culture. Their villages had been destroyed and their inhabitants scattered. No one knew what would come next. They were scared to move into Turkey, scared to return to Iraq. Some had been pushed into Syria. Some would inevitably immigrate to Europe and America.

They were looking for a savior and America fit the bill, but America is a fickle friend and it was worrying to see them attach so much to a power that is spread so thin. So, as the camp became increasingly familiar, as subjects became friends, and as their causes became my own, it also became clear how these individuals might be transmuted into mere refugees. They would be cared for by NGO's and host states like Turkey, and sooner or later the world would forget about them.

If they were lucky they would become a protected minority, but they would not enjoy equal rights. And their life prospects would be diminished. It seemed the glow of hope that sometimes follows in the wake of disaster might quickly turn to despair as they passed from front page news to a back page story and on into the occasional National Geographic special interest item.

Ishmael and another Yezidi friend Sivan both agreed that it was more important for them to live than to save their culture. It was a refreshing and broad-minded sentiment. And yet a culture should provide the means to live, and in making the Yezidis into refugees and destroying their culture, these bright young people had now been forced to make their way in life on their own, without the benefit of a community of support. Some would perhaps soar, many would fall by the wayside, but each of them deserves the chance, and for that they will need a safe way out of the camps and some semblance of a culture that might provide mutual support.

THE NAZIS ARE BACK ON
THE FIRST STOP TO EUROPE

The brass swastika rested on the table, a grandiose war-eagle perched above, as passersby strolled the balmy avenue, wending their way past quiet cafés on the road to the Acropolis. Comfortable in his bigotry, the old man tending the stall dismissed my incomprehensible abuses with a practiced wave of the hand. Perhaps it had something to do with the electoral success of Golden Dawn, the Greek neo-Nazi party, which had recently taken nine-percent of the vote; or maybe it was because their biggest constituency was the police force itself.

Greece is a beautiful country, which entered the modern-era in the early nineteenth century when Ukrainian intellectuals began to talk about breaking away from the Ottoman Empire and stoked the imaginations of European dreamers. Like so many nations, it was born in the mind and backed by the military might of great powers. The revolution was the cause celebré of Europe in the 1820's, and Lord Byron, the romantic poet, even fought and died in its now forgotten struggle.

Yet, the state was born into a crippling debt, which was not paid-off until the twentieth century. From the start, it followed a boom-bust cycle of growth and decline in which, for some time following the two world wars, people even spoke of the Greek Miracle.[141] But the state was now in a down-cycle, brought on by reckless borrowing, government corruption, and the stranglehold of creditors.

Athens can be an incredibly warm and human-scale city, made magical with ancient ruins, but it has also taken on in many places the appearance of a third-world country. Most shops in the neighborhood where we stayed appeared abandoned, much of the block looked bombed out. Several of the buildings were in a state of disrepair not much better than the ancient Athenian ruins, and the economic decline portended a deeper despair of the spirit.

Greece has recently become the first stop for refugees on the road to Europe as well. Syrians, Iraqis, Afghanis – the victims of war and genocide – stream in on blow-up rafts, tossed on the wine-dark sea, like Odysseus struggling to find land. They too are the victims of epic battles, with their own odysseys no doubt waiting to be crafted into verse. Most are shuttered away in camps, where my partner trains teachers on how to work with trauma. But refugees also dot some of the busier streets, and we were told neo-Nazis often beat them up.

Greece's second largest city of Thessaloniki was almost half-Jewish prior to the Second World War, when over 80 percent of the country's Jews were murdered in the Nazi occupation.[142] Thousands fought the Nazi invaders, side-by-side with Greeks, in a war that would ravage the country, but the Greek fascists of today, who mimic their invaders, somehow think themselves patriotic.

Neo-Nazis are not the brightest bunch. In a bid to outdo the confusion of their compatriots at home, a handful followed Lord Byron's romantic example and travelled to Syria to fight for the Assad regime. There they joined the jihadists of Hezbollah and the Iranian National Guard in the killing of secular democratic revolutionaries in the deluded belief they were fighting Islamist terrorists. Of course, there were plenty of jihadists among the rebels, so perhaps this was often true. But more often than not, they were working hand-in-glove with their own adversaries. Perhaps they were more drawn to Vladimir Putin, now assisting the regime in its genocide of Aleppo. The Russian Nazis, whom Putin tacitly supports, comprise about half the world's total and also like to think of themselves as patriotic – in spite of the Nazi invasion of Russia killing 20 million.

Jews may not think themselves related to Syrian refugees, but not so long ago they were the ones suffering genocide at the hands of Nazis. Now the Muslims have occupied their old European social niche. From Hamburg to Haifa, Arabs are the new Jews. Hence, the neo-Nazis of Greece are also tacit allies in a way with the American-Israel lobby, which has been propagating Islamophobic arguments for decades. And the European right, which used to attack the Jews, is now attacking Muslims instead. It is all softer and more twenty-first century, with the only gas chambers being in the bathrooms – decked out with fancy tiles and softer hues – but the fascism is real enough.

While most think of Greece as foundational to Western civilization, it can often appear uncannily Eastern. The Greeks were the first people to break away from the Ottoman Empire. Later, the Lebanese and Egyptians, Iraqis and Syrians, would follow. My partner, whose roots are Lebanese, points out an array of similarities between Greece and Lebanon. The walking center of the city, the leisurely way of relating, the rocky outcrops and seaside inlets, even the comfort with stagnation and corruption, all betray Greece's roots in the former Ottoman Empire.

Visitors have been traveling to Greece for a couple hundred years now expecting an encounter with the West only to be met with these paradoxes. Perhaps they have just been coming with the wrong set of expectations. But it is ironic to see the Greeks taking such a liking to Nazism, given the extent to which German Nazis devastated their country. And it is even more astonishing, given that the movement is largely a response to a more recent economic devastation also brought on by German hatred, this time of a gentler and more technocratic sort. But as is the case in so many other places, there is nothing more common than for victims to assume the roles of their perpetrators.

Refugees report to us that most Greeks have been wonderful and welcoming. The Lebanese have similarly opened their arms to Syrian refugees, who now constitute an unbelievable quarter of their population. And this reminds me of a video taken some time back of children in Gaza – which is now suffering a ten year siege and is often referred to as the most densely populated place in the world.

The children were asked how they felt about taking in a million Syrian refugees, and in the best Arab tradition of hospitality, one-by-one they exclaimed it their duty and the neighborly thing to do. Even when pressed over their population concerns and lack of resources, they nevertheless persisted. Perhaps Bob Dylan got it right. "When you ain't got nothing,' you got nothing to lose."

It was in this same spirit that the great powers of Europe once helped Greece fight a revolution and later brought them into their new European Union. Perhaps we all have a lot to learn from the children of Gaza.

THE BEIRUT BOMBING
WE JUST MISSED

The small Beirut neighborhood, where we had been walking, was rocked by two Isis suicide bombs just half an hour after we were whisked away by a cab driver who had spent a quarter of a century fighting for Hezbollah. The neighborhood was Shia and a Hezbollah stronghold. The bomb blasts left 43 people dead, many of whom we had probably just passed on the streets. We spent some time contemplating the people who died and how it could have been us: they were poor and simple, with seemingly strong community ties. The vast majority were merely the unlucky victims of wider political forces, but the event itself probably seemed closer to our friends back home, who saw footage of the aftermath on television.

It was the day before the much more widely publicized Paris attacks – which would contribute to France almost electing a far-right fascist – but the Lebanese bombing could have turned out to be just as consequential. Lebanon has maintained a remarkable degree of stability amid a wave of refugees streaming in from next door in Syria. The refugees now make up an incredible 20-25 percent of the population. They are spread across hundreds of camps and often integrated into the wider society, so everyone gives us a different answer as to how many are actually living in the country. But they are hurting the economy and may soon strain Lebanon's notoriously fragile balance of power. Meanwhile, the Lebanese militia, Hezbollah, has been fighting in Syria, and the attack we barely missed may have pulled them in more deeply.

Lebanon has long resisted definitions. Its political system is often referred to as a *confessional democracy*. There are Christians, Sunnis, Shia, and Druze, and each are awarded a proportionate number of seats in Parliament.[143] The system encourages strong religious identification, and while it tends to result in a high level of corruption and political patronage, it also holds the country together by giving everyone a stake.[144]

Lebanese politicians manage the tensions inherent in the system by stealing the state's resources instead of governing, but it is often forgotten that long before the Arab Spring, Lebanon was a beacon of democracy and the literary jewel of the Arab of world.[145] The benefits of democracy can be sensed in the way most everyone has their own political opinions and no one has anything good to say about the government. Lebanon is a sort of libertarian failed-state, in which a government stymied by ethnic divisions does little, but somehow the center holds.

As Hezbollah has grown in strength, it has become increasingly essential to Lebanon. While it began as a terrorist organization, resisting the Israeli occupation of southern Lebanon in the eighties, it soon came to constitute a disciplined fighting force, known for its principled and highly effective tactics. Over the decades it developed a multitude of social programs to lift Lebanon's oppressed Shia from poverty, and with the help of Iranian arms transfers through Syria, Hezbollah had pushed Israel from almost all of its small slice of occupied Lebanon by the year 2000.[146] Since that time it has become stronger than the Lebanese army itself, with which it often coordinates.

Lebanon somehow manages to defy Max Weber's classic definition of the state as the group possessing a monopoly of force in a given territory, but exceptions have a way of reverting to the norm over time.

Hezbollah's leader, Hassan Nasrallah, announced his strong support for the Assad regime in 2011, shortly after the pro-democracy protests began, and affirmed that support in 2013. It was a highly controversial move for a leader known to operate on principle, given the political suppression and extreme war crimes of the Assad regime. But Hezbollah was dependent upon the regime for Iranian arms transfers, without which they might suffer a massive decline in power. But even as their leader swore allegiance to the Assad regime, the Hezbollah fighters and supporters with whom we spoke claimed they were simply protecting Lebanon from extremists. This was what the cab driver, who drove us from the site of the bombing said. He may have driven like a terrorist, but he invited us to his home like a friendly villager. He told us that Hezbollah, with whom he fought in Syria, was not fighting the pro-democracy rebels but only Isis and the most extreme jihadi militias. It struck me as the kind of moral tale good people tell themselves when they are driven by circumstance to commit evil deeds, in this case genocide.

The Islamic State in Iraq, which was an early precursor of Isis, sought to sow sectarian divisions in areas of chaos. They pitted Sunni against Shia through suicide attacks, like the one we just missed, and in so doing tore apart American occupied Iraq, along with much of today's Syria. If Hezbollah were to overreact, Isis could do the same to Lebanon, but Lebanon has been here before. Taking on Hezbollah on their home turf may be a bit like a gang of punks challenging the Italian mafia in the Bronx. Hezbollah is the only military force to have pushed Israel from occupied territory, after all. Thus far the bombing seems to be pulling the country together, but it might just as easily inspire a wave of home-grown Sunni terrorism that eventually tears it apart. While Isis is quite foreign to cosmopolitan Lebanon, and enjoys virtually no support whatsoever, Hezbollah does not fair much better among Lebanese Sunnis. It is possible Isis will not gain a foothold in Lebanon but nevertheless succeed in pitting Lebanese Sunni and Shia against each other. If the Syrian refugees settling in Lebanon do not pass on to Europe or back to Syria, they may present still other challenges in eventually straining Lebanon's fragile demographic balance.

Hezbollah may be keeping Isis extremists out of Lebanon, but they might just as well be bringing them in. They are in this sense in much the same boat as Western leaders, who may also soon find themselves allied with an Assad regime responsible for perhaps an order of magnitude more deaths than the relatively poorly armed Isis. They would all do well to heed the wisdom of the Tao Te-Ching, which suggests ruling a state is like cooking small fish: the slightest indelicate move might easily tear it apart. If 9-11 taught us anything it is that terrorism is dependent on overreactions. The whole world would now do well to take a deep collective breath.

EIGHTY MILLION MUSLIMS
MISSING FROM EUROPE

Negotiating Antalya's highways at night is a bit like streaming through high mountain rapids.

The rules of the road are suspended, as cars glide from lane to lane and the mind turns to liquid. And yet, the signs of development are everywhere evident in the quality of automobiles and the roads upon which they drive. Turkey is becoming increasingly urbanized, increasingly developed, increasingly European, and, up until a few short years ago, increasingly democratic. And yet, it seems somehow to drift further and further away, like the lone man swimming out past the dock from which these words are written.

This is now my fourth journey to Turkey, and each time it seems to become more and more inaccessible, as if there is some window to the West that is slowly closing. Relatively strong development seems to have done little to integrate Turkey into the developed world. If anything, it is just the opposite.

The hotel staff seem resentful of their wealthy European and Russian patrons, and there is a palpable lack of openness to our differences. It is as if being on the margins of Europe for too long has brought about a souring. And there seems little room for a friendly smile or a few words of interest to heal the divide. Like inequality within nations, inequality between nations can be humiliating.

In contrasting the commonplace with the novelty of the unknown, travel has long been known to evoke new insights. Seeing these disparities up close makes them all the more poignant. And it sheds a new light on what many have experienced as a clash of civilizations, which might just as well be a clash of modes of production. What appear to be great cultural divides are all-too-often merely developmental divides and almost completely vanish after a generation or two of sustained economic growth. But these speculations on Turkey are little more than just that, for our contact with people has been slight thus far.

Here in Antalya, they are preparing for an upcoming G-20 summit. The progress they are making on the roads is happening too fast, as if none of it is meant to last. It reminds my partner and I of the film, *Risky Business*, where after a weekend of partying with prostitutes, Tom Cruise dashes through his house cleaning up any signs of abnormality just before his parents get home.

They are wiping the streets clean of any sign that this may still be a poor country in which hundreds of honor killings take place each year; in which democratic rights are being fast eroded by an elected but nevertheless authoritarian government; in which the southeastern Kurds, which were cleansed from thousands of villages in the nineties, and comprise about 20 percent of the population, still remain poorly integrated at best. The former Ottoman Empire, of which Turkey remains but a rump, was a powerful entity that would have rivaled any European state of its day. But Turkey itself has a long way to go before it possesses the feeling of a well-ordered, European democracy.

And yet, Turkey is, if anything, a place of contrasts: East and West, rich and poor, secular and religious, democratic and authoritarian, the divisions here can be sharp. Perhaps it is these contrasts that make it one of those places continually eluding the grasp of commentators since well before the twentieth century.[147] Being my first Islamic travel destination at age 18, where my connection with a local best friend and girlfriend ran deep, it has long held a special place in my heart. But however many books read and visits made, it still feels far away.

Turkey has long been known as the bridge between East and West. Lying in the heartland of the old Ottoman Empire, it is one of the world's largest Islamic states. And yet, just a few short years ago it seemed poised to become one of the largest states in the European Union. Following a long phase of expansion, in which its boundaries pushed outward into former Soviet territories, the E.U. now seems due for retrenchment, though, and the potential membership of Turkey may be the greatest casualty.

Turkish membership in the E.U. would add to it another 80 million person country to rival the U.K., France, and Germany. In so doing, it would add to Europe a vast influx of young workers, who might bolster the economy as population ages. In this way, Turkish membership could maintain the tax base as an older generation of Europeans pass into retirement. Turkish membership in the E.U. might, in this way, go a long way toward saving the European welfare state.

But the real problem with Turkey's entry is Islamophobia. Europeans committed genocide against their largest minorities, the Jews and Romani. And it can sometimes seem as if Muslims have simply been inserted in their place—another large minority, ill-integrated and problematic as before. Europe too needs to get its act together.

More Muslims in Europe will bring increasing exposure to both their similarities and differences, making the once unfamiliar familiar and breeding new fusions and possibilities for art, literature, culture, and community. This is how people have long learned to live together in peace, but it might just as easily intensify the backlash. Meanwhile, Turkey drifts between East and West, like the new cars, driving well designed roads, that cannot seem to settle on a lane. If it can find its place, it just might possibly heal the perceived divide between Islam and the West. Unfortunately, Turkey seems, much like Europe, to be driving itself down a fascist ravine, and it is only getting worse with each passing year.

WHATEVER HAPPENED
TO THE YEZIDIS

Isis fighters were streaming in fast and people were fleeing in every direction. Haidar rushed to his father's house to grab a pickup truck, which he quickly filled with the 20 members of two families. Then he raced at top speed to the Syrian border along a bumpy road, with genocidal fighters following close behind. But then something unexpected happened. He heard the voice of his four-year old daughter Yuva calling out. She had fallen from the truck, and landed on her head, and he was staring transfixed in the rearview mirror as she lay there in the road. His son was yelling to stop, but going back would mean risking the lives of 19 people. It is moments like these that define a man's life. The Islamic State routinely rapes the girls it kidnaps, so as he closed his eyes and pressed the pedal to the floor, one can only imagine what went through his mind.

Later he would be thanked for saving so many lives, but in relating this nightmare to my friend who was translating, he was devastated. This is what happens when a people is targeted for genocide. The brutality of Isis is stunning, and nightmares like these are quite common to come across among the Yezidis. But while almost nobody knew who they were but a few months ago, they are now mostly forgotten.

The Yezidis passed from being citizens to refugees, from fifteen minutes of fame to anonymity, and somehow we assume they are now secure. But the cauldron of violence we call the Middle East is no place to be a small, persecuted minority, with no outside protectors. Tens of thousands of Yezidis were almost slaughtered on

Mt. Sinjar because the fleeing Kurdish army, the Peshmerga, did not stop to alert them that Isis was heading their way. So, the Yezidis watched their protectors pass through their villages with little idea of the horrors that were to follow, and the ones who spoke to me about it in the camp felt nothing but disgust for the soldiers who were so willing to sacrifice their lives without muttering a word.

Now this same army is overseeing their refugee camps in northern Iraq. Yezidis from my earlier visit to a camp in Turkey, along with an aid worker working in one of these camps, report terrible conditions. Residents are served only a single meal a day, and they report local Kurds saying the Yezidis got what they deserved, by which they presumably mean the loss of all their assets, the annihilation of their communities, and the murder of their families. The Yezidis are still in crisis, still in danger, and these are the same Kurdish forces the U.S. is now arming.

Support for the Peshmerga is not an entirely amoral choice, though. The Assad government in Syria is easily the most genocidal state power in the world today. Backing them would mean support for their systematic starvation of cities and slaughter of prisoners. The Shia militias in Iraq are committing their own atrocities, and given the brutality to which they have been exposed, might easily morph into their own instantiation of radical hate. And the Iraqi army is weak, far too weak to take on Isis alone. About the only force that comes away looking clean is the PKK, a former communist, Kurdish group, that until just a couple of weeks ago was listed by the U.S. State Department as a terrorist organization. But one suspects that over time they will not outperform their reputation.

Isis has left all too many of us transfixed, and the refugees are now getting lost in the shuffle. One young Yezidi, who has kept in touch, is continually shifting from a better run Turkish camp back to Iraq, where he seeks underpaid work as a computer programmer. He is desperately trying to get out of the Middle East and wonders whether he has been forgotten.

The Yezidis are surrounded by peoples with whom they do not identity. One man from my visit to the camp joked about how when he would go to market to sell his eggs, the Muslims would not buy them because he was Yezidi. But he would remind them, he tells me with a laugh, that it was the chickens and not he who had laid the eggs. That he had to tell the joke reminds us of the endemic discrimination the Yezidis suffered. That he could joke about it with them at all reminds us that open discrimination need not break into outright persecution.

Yet, it is a tenuous toleration that can easily evaporate in times of war, and the Middle East is now more insecure for minorities than ever. Yezidi friends from the camp talk of fellow villagers, with whom they were living in peace, even friendship, who turned on them and joined Isis. They could give no distinguishing character-istic of which ones had joined, signaling a support reaching far past religious extremists. For most Yezidis there is now no going back to the way it was before.

America bears a special responsibility to the Yezidis, who wel-comed American troops in 2003 and often served in the military as soldiers and translators. It is difficult to imagine that this did not play some role in their being targeted by the Islamic State, which arose through militias aligned against the U.S. during the early stag-es of the Iraq War. Yezidis speak with enthusiasm about coming to America. They would be a small, easy to assimilate minority.

They also speak of immigrating to Israel, where there is a sub-stantial population of Jews, who were also pushed out of Iraq. A Yezidi told me today that in Sweden, where he now resides, and in Germany, where he lived for 10 years, the Yezidis are being welcomed personally and taken care of by the state. But Yezidi numbers are small – only half a million from Iraq – so they require special attention, and it is just these very numbers that make them so vulnerable. It is time to give the Yezidis the chance to go where they might prosper.

PART VI

GENOCIDE IN THE SUMMER OF HATE

GENOCIDE IN THE SUMMER OF HATE

Running from house to house in search of a place to hide, I reflected on how I had become the target of a genocidal hit squad. Isis was hunting me down, and not only were they known to kill, they were known to quite literally crucify their victims. So, as I slipped away into the inner recesses of an abandoned house, I began to wonder if my hiding place would soon become my tomb. My body trembled with terror as I imagined all of the ways it might be dissembled. Then, unlike so many others, I awoke from the nightmare. I awoke from the nightmare and reflected on the contingency of my own existence.

It is difficult to imagine what it would be like to be the victim of a genocide. Most of us cannot imagine it happening to our own people. If we could imagine it, we would likely suppress the thought, because it is just too horrifying to sustain. Each time a genocide broke out in the twentieth century, the people most likely to draw attention to it could not believe the reports. Word leaked out slowly, and millions died for lack of better awareness.[148] The ability to imagine being the victim of mass murder can help to stop it, but genocides tend to go unchecked largely because it is so difficult to imagine ordinary people carrying them out.

We cannot imagine the Hutus of the village assembled in a field to carry out the day's killing. We cannot imagine the face behind the mask of an Isis gunmen. Rather, when we hear about a genocide breaking out, we tend to drift into a haze of abstractions, counting the dead and bemoaning its senselessness. But genocides need to be understood if they are to be stopped, and perhaps the most difficult thing about understanding genocide is comprehending how someone might engage in it. So, it is also imperative we understand the process of committing genocide from the inside out.

My own experience of mass murder may sound trite, even ridiculous, but it may also shed some light on the deeper psychological dynamics at play. It did not involve the murder of humans or even animals, but rather of colorful caterpillars that bled a luminous green slime. I was seven and had collected dozens of the caterpillars in a garbage can lid. I am not sure exactly why I was collecting the caterpillars – perhaps it was because of their beauty, or maybe the idea of killing them all was gestating somewhere deep in my mind. But when the lid was full, I did not know what to do with them. So, as they crawled about and wiggled in circles, I began to smash their writhing little bodies. I can still recall my feeling of queasiness and sense of remorse at destroying these lives that had so enchanted me just moments before, but the killing continued, as if driven on by its own momentum.

Most genocides involve collecting human bodies. Often they will be moved from place to place without planning. The perpetrators want to get rid of them, but murdering them does not always seem to be the first thing on their minds. Sometimes they leave their victims out in the open to die. Sometimes they collect them in concentration camps. Yet, it is difficult to feed and shelter so many people, so as conditions worsen and bodies become emaciated, and as they begin to smell of excrement and fear, the perpetrators must start to see their victims as something less than human. It is harder to feel for masses than individuals, so the grouping of bodies makes the killing easier, and once it gets started, it feeds on itself, with each machete blow or shot in the head further dampening the killers' conscience.

Most histories of genocide focus on the intent that lays behind the genocide itself. But there is another way to tell the tales. The Nazis created and filled the concentration camps before they planned on killing all of their inhabitants, and Serbs had been starving and picking off civilians in the streets of Sarajevo for years before their genocidal massacre of over 8,000 men in Srebrenica. What were the causal links between the first and last killings, and how were the minds of the killers transformed in the process of the killing?

The Israeli novelist and peace activist, David Grossman, has written about an innocence that is lost when violence is used to break the skin. It is as if some line has been crossed that separates the abuse from that of ordinary affairs. Genocides often happen amid the trauma of war. Something dies inside of those who have seen their friends dying all around them and who have themselves become killers. Soldiers are often seized by the terror of death, a sensation that most of us are able to suppress in our day-to-day lives, but which breaks into the open in the fog of war. Because of the way it shatters the illusion of permanence, death can be enchanting and mesmerizing, and under the hypnotic trance of collective trauma, it simultaneously magnetizes and repels.[149]

This explains the cheering crowds of Israelis, lined up on the border of Gaza as their government wipes out whole neighborhoods, and it explains the popularity of war movies. But it also explains our inability to bring ourselves to peer into the mass graves. There is always a risk we will be pulled under into the world of the dead, as if mobbed by zombies. War has a way of turning all social mores on their heads, but war comes with its own set of limitations. Genocide tears away the mask of social restraint, and in the process destroys victims and perpetrators alike.

Somehow, we have again ripped off the mask. The numbers of dead in both Gaza and the Central African Republic have been minuscule compared to the great genocides of the twentieth century. Even the numbers of those killed by Isis and Assad, while vastly greater, are still relatively small. But the killing in each of these places has appeared to some observers as genocidal. Part of the numbers' paradox lies in the fact that, unlike in the twentieth century, the whole world is now watching. So, it is possible that what we are seeing is a highly restrained form of genocidal intent, but it is also quite possible that we have become more sensitized to the death of strangers and learned to pressure those who would otherwise commit genocide. Perpetrators may fear being taken to international courts, and the retributory cycle of violence may only just be scaling up.

Perhaps too, those who might commit genocide have come to see themselves through the eyes of the world. There is an emerging global ethic of restraint that is appearing everywhere in times of war, and this ethic of restraint is beginning to be enshrined in an emerging body of international law. So the would-be killers not only see themselves through the eyes of the world, but through the eyes of the world, they look to the courts and fear for their futures. Perhaps next time when we peer into the mass graves we will see not only the bodies of the individuals who have been killed, not only the faces of human lives now ended, but the very death of genocide itself.

GENOCIDE WILL EXPLODE
IN THE AGE OF TRUMP

The city of Sarajevo is contained by the mountains like some great cup, filled up at night with smog. It is a tolerant city where the Muslim call to prayer can be heard on the steps of a Catholic Church, a former Ottoman outpost where the Middle East blends effortlessly into the West. The people here appear introverted and calm, soft and open, and it is one of the most poignantly beautiful places to which I have travelled.

But back in the nineties, Sarajevo was the site of a three-year starvation siege in which civilians were picked off in the streets by Serbian snipers perched in the mountains. Western leaders did nothing to stop the genocide for years until NATO intervened in 1995 in a short bombing campaign that lifted the siege. Then peace returned, with the establishment of a rather precarious, corrupt but multi-ethnic and democratic state.[150]

It was arguably the first time America engaged militarily in a humanitarian intervention to stop genocide or ethnic cleansing.[151] The U.S. would do so again when the same Serbian regime threatened ethnic cleansing in Kosovo in 1999; when Libya's deputy representative to the U.N. warned that Gaddafi might commit genocide in 2011; and when tens of thousands of Yezidis were trapped by Isis on Mt. Sinjar in Iraq in 2014.

There were successes like Bosnia and failures like Libya, and the motives were often mixed. America and other Western states often did little if anything to stop mass murder in places like Darfur and Syria. But where American intervention was lacking, Britain,

France and the U.N. often filled the void, as in the narrowly averted genocide in the Central African Republic in 2014.

Enter President-elect Trump, a man who wonders why if we have them we do not use nuclear weapons; a man who sees no problem with nuclear proliferation; a man who is as unpredictable as he appears irrational; and mass murder is exploding in hotspots the world over.

The day after Trump talked with Putin, following his election, Russia announced an all-out assault on the remaining areas of rebel-held Syria. But the bombing of civilians in East Aleppo had already reached genocidal proportions, with regular attacks on hospitals and a siege that had left a population of 250,000 on the brink of starvation. The Obama administration may have ignored its own red lines concerning the use of chemical weapons, it may have let half-a-million people starve under regime sieges, but few expected it to stand by amid an all-out genocide. Yet, with Trump as President, Putin and Assad could go about their business with neither censure nor threat.

Attacks on the Rohingya in Burma also stepped up immediately following his election, with reports of children being thrown in fires and women being mass-raped—and this is no coincidence. In a stunning diplomatic achievement, the Obama administration successfully enticed one of the world's most repressive military regimes to open up and democratize. But in the process, its military leaders, who remained autonomous, increased attacks on the Rohingya—Burma's most defenseless minority—whom the U.N. has called "the world's most forgotten people."

Now that Trump will be president, the military can go about their business of subverting democracy through ethnic cleansing with neither censure nor threat. We should brace ourselves for something similar in Yemen. Britain and Obama armed Saudi Arabia in their fight against Houthi rebels in Yemen, and that fight involved starvation sieges and the bombing of agricultural facilities. The U.N. stated in the fall of 2016 that 7 million people were on the brink of starvation, but when the Saudis targeted political leaders attending a wedding, killing 140 civilians, Obama met them with a harsh rebuke and threatened a thorough review of American support. Weeks later, the Saudis were participating in a desperately needed cease-fire and America was limiting arms sales. But with Trump as president, they can go about their business with neither censure nor threat; and there will be other brutal attacks in the Middle East as well.

Israel has carried out increasingly brutal bombing campaigns on Gaza every couple of years for the last decade or so, and the last attack in 2014 involved the targeting of schools and civilian kill-zones in which anything that moved was to be shot. Meanwhile, prominent Israeli leaders began talking about Palestinians as snakes that needed to be killed in the womb. But with a couple of thousand civilian deaths, the attack did not reach genocidal proportions, and this probably had a lot to do with the unpredictability of the American response. It will be different when Trump is president.

Genocides tend to break out when no one is looking. They explode in times of war and nationalist fervor. They erupt when people feel insecure and lash out against outsiders. They overflow when the world is in chaos.[152] Times like the Second World War, times like the fall of the Soviet Union, times like that of today. Trump will bring chaos to the world. He will bring a sense of disorder and lawlessness, and he has already made it well-known that he does not care.

The period from 1995 to 2015 has been a remarkably peaceful period of human history, extensively documented in Steven Pinker's, *Better Angels of Our Nature*.[153] But it can seem just the opposite for America watchers, who tend rather to see in this period an ever-intensifying era of military engagements. What we all-too-often miss is that while America has been busy starting senseless conflicts like the Iraq War, and humanitarian interventions like in Libya, the rest of the world remained relatively quiet.

It is one of the unfortunate ironies of history that life is often most peaceful under the boot of empires. A clear balance of power invites stability, and a single hegemon can set others to rest. But when the balance of power is in flux and many vie for dominance, things can get bloody. For war breaks out where power vacuums abound; when states underestimate the strength and resolve of rivals; and when great powers proliferate.[154]

The age of American decline, which many mark with the Great Recession, was perhaps always bound to be brutal. Foreign policy analysts have been arguing for years now that we have shifted from a unipolar to a multipolar world,[155] and such a world will be filled with war.[156] As America loses resolve, others powers like Russia and China are filling the power vacuum, and everywhere it seems states are testing the boundaries of the international order.

But the election of Trump has signaled the end of any predictable order whatsoever. We should expect it to be violent, bloody, unpredictable, and dangerous. And the ones who will be hit the hardest are the most vulnerable, like the Rohingya, the Palestinians, the Yemeni's, and the Syrians in East Aleppo. Genocides will explode in the age of Trump and we will be picking up the pieces for generations to come.

MURDEROUS MONKS
AND SILENT SANGHAS

His Facebook account is almost certainly hacked by the government and his life has already been threatened three times by Buddhist mobs. The last time, five men approached him with sticks, and he barely escaped on his bicycle. It is not uncommon for Muslims to be beaten to death by small gangs of Buddhists in Burma. So, he wants me to get my article out as soon as possible in case he is killed. Sometimes our nightly chats on Facebook remind me of the beginnings of a spy movie, as we endlessly discuss how we can smuggle him across borders and win him asylum.

Kyaw Kyaw Win is a village leader for the National League for Democracy. His is the party of Aung San Suu Kyi, winner of the Nobel Peace Prize and often considered the Nelson Mandela of Burma. But Kyaw Kyaw is not only an activist, he is a Muslim and half-Rohingya. The two together in Burma can be a deadly concoction. Suu Kyi is not in a position to speak out in favor of the rights of Muslims, who are increasingly the victims of persecution, and it is unclear whether or not she cares. Her party is under threat and losing popular support, as the ruling generals coordinate with respected Buddhist monks, who whip mobs into a nationalist fury.

But while excuses might be made, it is sad and disheartening to see such a moral authority failing to speak out on such an important issue. The only thing people in the developed world tend to know about countries like Burma are their moral leaders like Suu Kyi and the terrors they resist,[157] making her failure to speak out a transformative moment for Burma itself. Her failure to speak out against these injustices will sully not only her own reputation but that of her country as well, thereby risking a loss of aid dollars and investments alike, which might spur on its own return to autocracy.

Run by a small body of generals for the last half century, Burma is one of the poorest countries in the world. Ever since independence from British rule in 1948, it has been riven with ethnic rebellions in its hinterlands. Leaders have see-sawed back and forth between granting autonomy to ethnic minorities and centralizing authority, but centralization has almost always carried the day.[158]

The centralization of power in Burma has long involved one of the world's most rigorous systems of censorship.[159] The censorship is so great that Burmese would, until quite recently, routinely risk their lives to provide little bits of information to foreigners traveling through the country. A friend of mine who traveled there as a tourist in the mid-2000s, for instance, told of a man who approached him to sell some art. After flipping through the man's drawings, he came to a page with a message asking my friend to tell the world about what is happening to the Burmese. Such stories were common in those days, but things have been looking brighter in the last few years.

As dictators across the Middle East were clamping down on Arab Spring activists, Burma's ruling *junta* was announcing their desire to open the country up and hold elections. Much the same thing had happened in 1990, when Suu Kyi won the Presidency. The results were not expected and were thus nullified by the generals. She was then put under fifteen years of on-and-off house arrest, which ended in 2010. While she is now free to lead her party, she has nevertheless been barred from running for office under a carefully crafted law that forbids office holding to people who are married to foreigners. There are always ways to manipulate a democratic system to game the results you want, but these abuses can be curbed over time, even for a fragile state like Burma.

While the country has opened up over the past few years, it has only made things worse for the minority Muslims. The process of democratization can expose social fissures that have long been covered over.[160] Perhaps the most contentious in Burma lies with the

Muslim Rohingya, who are now being ethnically cleansed. While they began migrating to Burma in the early nineteenth century, they have often passed back and forth into bordering Bangladesh and have never been integrated into the countries' majority Buddhist population.[161] Swamping population centers in the coastal Arakan state, they have long been resented by locals, who have now had enough.

The Muslim Rohingya are stateless refugees. The United Nations says they are one of the most oppressed peoples in the world. Buddhist leaders in Burma accuse them of having ties to Al-Qaeda. But while numerous mountain ethnic groups have remained in a near constant state of armed rebellion since independence, the Rohingya have been far more peaceful. Still, the mobs that hunt them have often raped the women and killed the men in a pattern typical of many ethnic cleansings and genocides.[162] And it is just such mobs that terrify my friend.

Perhaps the most surprising thing about these mobs is that they are spurred on by monks. Friends report that the Buddhist sangha, or community of monks, is sharply divided over these persecutions. Throughout its history, monks in Burma have tended to be highly political. Prior to British colonialism, they often set the conditions for state power, and they played a leading role in resisting both the British and the later *junta* of generals. In much the same way late twentieth-century Islamism tended to arise in places where people living under dictatorships could only organize in the mosques, monks have often played a leading role in Burma's political resistance by organizing in the monasteries.[163] But as the democratization process exposes the inner fault lines of Burmese society, these same monks are increasingly turning to nationalism.

Buddhist teachers outside of Burma have spoken out against this violence. A letter signed by Thich Nhat Hanh and the Dalai Lama, among others, urged the Burmese sangha to abide by Buddhist teachings of nonviolence. Another signed by 381 American Buddhist teachers, urged President Obama to raise the issue, which he did, in his recent trip to Burma. But the murderous monks of Burma seem far more active than the silent sanghas of the world.

Buddhists have long remained immune to the withering criticism of religion that is often expounded upon by a new breed of atheists intent on exposing religiosity itself as a mythological excuse for domination and aggression. It would be a shame to see them direct their bitterness at Buddhists as well, and for all the right reasons. While Burma has a sizable population of 53 million people, few people outside of the region know much about what is happening there. Theravadan Buddhists could do much to expose this issue and pressure the monks and government. Most have instead sat silently—not even observing the suffering. They would do well to lend some of the attention they give to observing their own suffering to that of the world as well.

THE SUFFERING BUDDHISTS
DON'T WANT TO HEAR ABOUT

The United Nations has described them as the world's most forgotten people and the crimes they suffer as genocide. They have endured mass rape and random killings. They have been pushed from their ancestral homeland and left to languish in refugee camps. They are hungry and thirsty and susceptible to disease, and they have been put in this condition all in the name of Buddhism.

The Rohingya are a tiny Muslim minority in the almost entirely Buddhist state of Burma, also known as Myanmar. Buddhist nationalists see them as a threat to their dominance. Buddhist monks have routinely led mob attacks on their villages. Almost half-a-million were just ethnically cleansed from the places of their birth. And it has been whitewashed away by Burma's de facto head-of-state, Aung San Suu Kyi, probably the world's most revered female Buddhist leader.

The ethnic cleansing of Rohingya must come as a rude awakening for those who have idealized Buddhist societies. But it is not the first time Buddhism has been used as the ideological tool of a genocidal army. Japan's most prominent Zen Masters provided the ideological justification for Emperor Hirohito's fascism in World War II, which arrogated vast portions of East and Southeast Asia and forced thousands of women into sex slavery.[164]

It would be as absurd to hold ordinary Buddhists responsible for these crimes against humanity, as it would be for Burmese Buddhists to hold the Rohingya responsible for those committed by Al-Qaeda in the name of Islam. A shared religious identity is one of the most powerful principles around which people can organize, so organized religions will probably always be prone to hijacking in the service of violence.[165] But it is for precisely this reason that the members of a religious community would do well to speak out against the crimes committed in their names.

American Buddhists tend to renounce organized religion, as if what they are doing is altogether different. But anyone who has ever managed a meditation center can tell you that teaching meditation requires vast resources. Classes must be taught someplace, teachers supported somehow, books published somewhere. Retreat centers are needed to deepen practice, for social events to hold the community together, and services to mediate life transitions. Moral rules are needed to preserve a sense of decency, and meditation center managers are needed to make it all run smoothly.

What began as a spiritual discipline is thus transformed into an organized religion, and there is little with which people identify so much as their religion. For religion binds us together around what matters most. It is a beautiful thing to make your closest relations those with whom you can share your deepest experiences. But once we become identified with a religious tradition, we become implicated in the lives of our co-religionists, thereby thrusting upon us special burdens of moral responsibility.

We become responsible for caring for fellow community members, for in the absence of such care spiritual disciplines would become mere exercises in narcissism. But we also become responsible for what is done in the name of the religion, for little is exploited so much as religion. And if the exploitation of a religion is allowed to carry on without censure, the religion itself will become a magnet for shysters and warmongers.

Serious spiritual traditions tend to inspire their practitioners to take on some such responsibilities and use them as grist for the mills of their own spiritual development. Spiritual practice encourages us to let go of self-centered attachments and see ourselves as part of something greater. This deepening sense of interconnectedness tends to inspire moral action and social service, for it deepens empathy and eases the burdens associated with moral responsibility. It is in short easier to give back to others when you have reduced your own attachments.

Western Buddhists are particularly well-placed to protect the Rohingya. Many, like myself, have an emotional tie to the country through having practiced under Burmese teachers. But all of us are tied to it through the practice of Buddhism itself, whose teachings are being used to justify the killings. By speaking out against ethnic cleansing in the name of Buddhism, we withhold from the leaders of the ethnic cleansing powerful ideological tools, and we draw into question the nature of the Buddhist identity that is being used to inspire violence. Moreover, since Buddhism is so strongly opposed to violence, we bring to the protection of the Rohingya the Buddha's own teachings on nonviolence.

Western Buddhists are also trained in the observation of suffering. We sit with it daily in our meditation practices and must often endure weeks of it at a stretch in intensive retreats. This makes us unusually well-suited to grapple with the suffering of the Rohingya. Few people can stare for long in the cold eyes of genocide. We become disheartened by the brutality of humanity, traumatized by the crimes to which we bear witness, and rapidly subject to burnout. Buddhist meditators, however, are trained in remaining unbound by the suffering they face, and most would do well to step outside their comfort zones and face it a bit more.

It is quite possible the monks leading mobs attacks on innocent Rohingya were brainwashed or planted by the military, which began controlling the monasteries after monks protested the regime en masse in 2007. But the Rohingya tend to be hated by most Burmese largely because they are not Buddhist. The hatred and attacks increased when the country democratized, for democratization always raises the question of who is in and who is out. Identity issues are interlaced through every element of these attacks.

It is, of course, ironic that Buddhists, whose practices focus on cutting through the illusion of a separate self, would make identity so central to their crimes against humanity. The dissolution of the self-sense is so central to Buddhism as to make anyone who would kill in the name of a more pure Buddhist national identity a sort of cosmic buffoon. But such misunderstandings are typical of the practitioners of any organized religion, which is why so many spiritual teachings are dedicated to combating just these sorts of distortions.

The leaders of a religious community bear special responsibility to speak out against moral wrongs committed in their names. They are especially responsible because, unlike most everyone else, their voices are likely to be respected and heard. And unlike most everyone else, speaking out is often astonishingly easy. It would take little effort for senior teachers associated with the Insight Meditation Center and the Vipassana Meditation Society, whose traditions are intimately tied to Burma, for instance, to lead their communities in condemning the violence.

Spiritual teachers are perhaps most responsible insofar as they represent their traditions. In this way, their silence is a form of assent, like the Bishops and Popes who failed to acknowledge the sexual abuse in their own tradition. The analogy is imperfect, for there is a wide world of Buddhist traditions, each with its own issues, and only one Catholic Church. But the analogy highlights the expectation that spiritual leaders should protect their religions from abuse and the ease with which others can get away with it when they abdicate responsibility.

Perhaps the most important thing we can do is simply proclaim that these people have fundamentally misunderstood their own religion and have nothing whatsoever to do with actual Buddhism. This protects the religion, isolates the protagonists, and undercuts their authority. So much the better if we donate to aid groups, sponsor children, serve in refugee camps, and publicly speak out against ethnic cleansing in petitions, posts, and articles. The Rohingya need someone to assure their basic human rights will be respected, and who better than those in whose name their rights are being violated?

GENOCIDE IS BEING GLOBALIZED ON SOCIAL MEDIA

Muslim Rohingya are being burned alive, gang raped, and beheaded in Burma right now.

If you think seeing is believing, you can peruse videos of Rohingya children being whipped as they stand in line waiting for food and Burmese undertakers walking through rows of countless bodies burnt to a crisp. If you are more apt to trust the research, you can peruse the endless testimonies compiled by groups like Amnesty[166] and Human Rights Watch.[167] Their reports tell of women being raped while the men are killed, hundreds of villages being burnt to the ground, an exodus of 600,000 Rohingya fleeing to refugee camps in Bangladesh, and hundreds of thousands of the people in those camps now starving. If you doubt the intent of the killers, you can simply look at what they have to say on the comment sections of mainstream news sites, where they have largely taken over. There they will tell you the women deserve to be raped, the refugee children look like pigs, and all Muslims should be killed. They post laughing emojis in response to articles on women being gang raped, and they mock the people who plea for their humanity.

Seldom if ever has a genocide involved so much mockery of its victims.

They are enabled by conservative Americans who support and share their views. The political affiliations of these Americans can be discerned by simply looking at their Facebook profiles. They are also enabled by Indians, who elected a prime minister a few years ago who, prior to the election, was principally known outside of India for having said nothing when mobs in the state where he was governor killed a couple thousand Muslims in a few days. Their principle argument is that because the Rohingya had a militia, which killed 30 police officers just prior to the start of the genocide, they are terrorists and got what they deserved. Never mind the fact that human rights organizations had been reporting similar crimes against the Rohingya long before they had a militia[168]; never mind the fact that ethnically cleansing over half-a-million people because a tiny, rogue portion of them attacked the police in retaliation borders on the sociopathic.

They also argue that there is no proof of the genocide. This sort of denial is typical when genocides first break out.[169] But this time we have the photos of hacked up bodies, the videos of burning villages, the reports from human rights organizations, and the testimony of journalists. However, few can imagine what actually takes place in a genocide, so when the perpetrators of genocide deny it is taking place, they actually gain an audience through the sheer insanity of their murderousness. Nobody could be so brutal to incinerate a whole race of people, after all—but, of course, they could be and often are.

Many of these people look like paid trolls: their profiles are thin, their friend lists minuscule. But many simply look like they are there to enjoy the bloodsport, and others still that they are engaging in a war of civilizations. They actually blame the Muslims for being attacked, arguing that because bad stuff is always happening to them, they must be to blame. It is common to let such things slide when they are said about Muslims, but just imagine the outcry if we were to blame the Holocaust on the Jews.

It was only the most jittery of critics who worried that supporters of President Trump and the Indian Prime Minister Modi would go genocidal—but somehow, they found a way to get in on the action. They may not smell the flesh of their victims and hear the cracking of their skulls, but they are participating in a genocide nonetheless. They are our fathers and brothers, sisters and mothers. They are ordinary Americans helping provide cover for the mass murder of Muslims that another people wants to keep out of their country; and while they are providing cover, they can see for themselves just how hateful their new comrades really are.

It is similar to what has been happening in Syria, though there it is far more visceral. Young men with sociopathic tendencies from across the world have been joining Isis so they might find a Yezidi "wife" they can rape on a regular basis. And young men from Iraq, Iran, and Lebanon have been joining militias to fight on the side of the Bashar al-Assad regime, which has now killed tens of thousands of prisoners, most of whom experienced severe and prolonged torture prior to their deaths. Now it appears that many American Trump supporters are beginning their own virtual globalized genocide.

These mobs are so unprecedented we have barely begun to call out their actions as genocidal. But a handful of specialists in the study of genocide have been arguing for decades now that on-the-ground research suggests people tend to engage in genocide not because they have been ordered to do so by authorities, but rather because they want to get in on the action.[170] And what we are seeing today is ordinary people getting in on the killing from afar. The angry crowds that once carried out local pogroms against Jews in Eastern Europe are now forging globalized virtual hit squads.

We have globalized what economists might call the genocidal value chain. A global value chain is made up of the steps needed to bring products to market. It includes the production of parts in distant places, their coming together in a single location for assembly, and their final distribution to points of sale. Genocides are now produced in much the same way. They are spurred on by local leaders and hit squads. They are backed by supportive governments, which provide the arms. They are justified by social media trolls. And they are protected by anti-imperial, peace activists. The genocide against Syrian dissidents would not have been possible without leftist conspiracy theorists muddying the debate, peace activists shifting the narrative from human rights abuses to Western interference, and Russian trolls making up lies on social media.

News sites could shut down this activity by simply making it more difficult for trolls to get on their comment sections and by setting up their own internal regulations against group libel, an older legal term for libel against whole groups of people, and incitement to violence against whole categories of people. The benefits would accrue not only to people in distant places but to their own most dedicated readers as well, who would reap the rewards of more reasonable discussion. But a more important step might involve simply calling it out for what it is, which is the aiding and abetting of genocide.

Somehow, we have normalized anti-social hate on social media. If we are to restore our humanity and reweave the fabric of our social lives, we would do well to consider the standards and norms we set for acceptable behavior and speech. A good place to start would be to cast support for genocide to the outer margins of social life.

OBAMA MUST QUIT YEMEN
OR RISK GENOCIDE UNDER TRUMP

Most Americans have only the faintest notion of the American drone war that has been raging in Yemen for the last six years. Fewer still are aware their government has been supporting a Saudi-led invasion of Yemen for almost two years running with arm sales and logistical support. And perhaps the best kept secret of all is that the Saudi attack and related fighting has led the World Food Program to declare 2.2 million Yemenis at risk of hunger, with half of them on the brink of famine.

Millions of Yemeni children are at risk of starvation, and according to UNICEF, a Yemeni child is already dying once every 10 minutes and at least 462,000 are suffering from "severe, acute malnutrition."[171] The world has not seen anything like this since the Ethiopian famine of the eighties, with countless images now emerging of barely human looking children, who under the best of circumstances will already be stunted for life.

The famine has grown slowly and imperceptibly amid the recent American elections and horrors of Aleppo and is now just breaking into public view. But the Obama administration and its British partners have known about it for months and have recently begun to rebuke the Saudis and pull some arm sales. However, America still helps the Saudi-led coalition of Arab states with intelligence, logistical support, pilot training, and helicopter sales.[172] If it is eventually found the Saudi attack on Yemen is genocidal in intent, then Obama officials may also be held accountable.

And there is good reason to believe this famine is not accidental.

Located at the southern end of the Arabian Peninsula, Yemen was divided into two countries until the end of the Cold War, when both states merged under the rule of Ali Abdullah Saleh, North Yemen's head-of-state since 1978. Its poverty and internal divisions made it a ripe target for Al-Qaeda operatives in the early 2000's, and the U.S. began assassinating them through targeted drone strikes in 2009.[173] America became further entrenched when the Arab Spring erupted in 2011 and Yemenis pushed out their leader in an internationally negotiated transition.[174] The government of Saleh then joined with what many believe to be Iranian backed Houthi rebels and America lent its support to the new administration of his former Vice-President, Abdrabbuh Mansour Hadi. That support increased when Houthi rebels took over the government and the Saudis invaded in the winter of 2015.[175]

It all sounded reasonable to many in the American foreign policy establishment at the time, as America was supporting an internationally backed government and democratic elections, while preventing the takeover of the country by dangerous jihadists. Moreover, Hadi hailed from the more liberal south, while the ousted Saleh came from the more tribalized north, where he often pitted the tribes against each other in a strategy of divide and conquer.[176] The Arab Spring remained almost wholly nonviolent in Yemen, and there were substantial moves toward the liberation of women. Finally, it was believed by many that a more rational and inclusive government might better grapple with the country's substantial existential challenges.

Yemen is the poorest country in the Middle East, with a poverty rate of over 50 percent. Prior to the Saudi invasion, the country already faced high population growth, food and water scarcity, economic stagnation, and widespread poverty.[177] And these have been exacerbated by a Saudi naval blockade, putatively meant to keep out arms but also preventing desperately needed food supplies from reaching the country, 90 percent of which are imported. Even when the food makes it through, Saudi destruction of critical infrastructure, like bridges and ports, makes it difficult to reach populations displaced by the fighting. The Saudis have assaulted cities, putting poverty stricken urban residents on the run in a country that is already resource poor. And they have targeted civilian gatherings, like a wedding party in which they killed 140.

The crisis in Yemen is complex, so it has been easy to treat the famine as a mere accident of war and consequence of state failure. But famines are seldom accidental and almost always preventable. Perhaps the world's foremost scholar of famines, Amartya Sen, a Nobel Laureate in Economics for his work on the issue, notes that famines are almost always political and easily preventable. When food is not reaching a population it is because the powers that be are either using it as a weapon or suppressing critical information relating to the famine. Sen is famous for having first noticed that no major famine has ever occurred in a democracy, arguing this is because information on the famine always gets out when there is freedom of speech and the press. The corollary is that famines have been quite common under colonial regimes, which may be the best way to think of what is happening in Yemen: foreign powers control the country and their backers at home are reluctant to view the famine as stemming from political causes.

Famine in Yemen seems less a consequence and more a weapon of war.[178]

Secretary of State Kerry has repeatedly pressed for cease-fire agreements, which would allow desperately needed aid to reach starving populations, but his efforts have been contradictory, pressing for cease fires while at the same time arming the most dangerous power. And they have been subverted by warring parties. It is difficult to imagine President Trump exercising the same caution and restraint. Far more likely, he simply will not care and will back the Saudis to the hilt. But if that is the case, he may find himself overseeing a full-on genocide with millions of children dying before the court of world opinion. If the Obama administration has contributed to the crisis reluctantly, Trump may do so wholeheartedly. And it is quite possible his business interests in Saudi Arabia will lead him to give the thumbs up to their most brutal tactics.

The idea that millions of people might up-and-die in a famine in this day and age might seem simply unimaginable. And this is how it may have appeared to Chinese officials in Mao's Great Famine, which killed 45 million from 1958 to 1962. Information from the countryside was suppressed or ignored, as irrational economic policies collapsed the rural economy and market for food. As reports of starvation rolled in, Chairman Mao drifted into denial amid a nightly orgy of hedonistic delights. He stopped tending to government business, even stopped bathing and brushing his teeth.[179]

If the Obama administration cannot end the fighting now by dropping support for Saudi Arabia, it is quite possible history will repeat itself in another country on the other side of the world, also upended by civil conflict and revolutionary changes. America is in crisis and Americans may simply ignore the famine amid an onslaught of pernicious legislation. It is quite possible if Trump has a conscience, he would drift into the same escapist denial as Mao. But Trump has shown little regard for life and has already praised several dictators who have committed genocide, from Saddam Hussein to Bashar Al-Assad. President Obama needs to quit Yemen now or risk America's first genocide of the twenty-first century under Trump.

IS TRUMP COMMITTING
GENOCIDE IN YEMEN?

While Trump has been busy distracting attention from the Russia in-quiry at home and shoring up his humanitarian credentials in Syria, his administration has been participating in a quiet effort to starve millions of Yemeni civilians into submission. The Saudi-led coali-tion waging war in Yemen, with the United States' full support, has been carrying out a bombing campaign that has made it virtually impossible for most of the country to feed itself.

The result is that a Yemeni child is starving to death once every 10 minutes, according to UNICEF.[180] But if this is the case, it means about 4,000 are dying each month and 48,000 a year, though no one seems to be performing this logical extrapolation. The death tolls of such tragedies typically grow to be vastly larger than the first esti-mates suggest, so with millions currently starving, we should expect the final death count to ultimately reach the hundreds of thousands. How it got to this point and what it means for the moral integrity of America may be the most neglected story of our time.

The U.S. initially entered Yemen through a quiet drone pro-gram in 2009 to combat the rise of a peculiarly powerful branch of al-Qaida. When Yemen was destabilized by Arab Spring protests in 2011 that sought to oust the nation's dictator of more than 30 years, America was instrumental in orchestrating a U.N.-supported democratic transition.[181] But the change of administrations did not go so well, calling to mind a Congolese expression more apt for what Yemen was about to experience. Yemen was in the throes of a "demonic transition."

A long-simmering rebellion by the Houthi ethnic minority managed to oust the new administration, and the Houthi then allied themselves with the former dictator, whom they had just been fighting. Then, in the poorest state in the Arab world, suffering from chronic food shortages and a dwindling water supply, with a youthful population afraid for the future of their already collapsing state, things really got bad.

The Houthis are Shia Muslims, which made Arab Sunnis uncomfortable. The climate of instability was perceived as a danger to Western states like the U.S. and U.K. Thus, they all joined together under Saudi leadership to put down the rebels and bring back the second internationally recognized government, who had been installed following the Arab Spring protests. The idea was that a less tainted regime might better stabilize the country and work with the West to put down al-Qaida militants.

Most Americans ignored what was happening under the quiet leadership of the Obama administration. For it seemed at the time to be a decent and sensible if somewhat questionable game. The only problem was that the Sunni Saudi regime was already engaged in a proxy war with Shiite Iran in Syria. The Iranians were working hand in glove with the regime of Bashar al-Assad, massacring mostly Sunni civilians in genocidal proportions and the Saudis were about to do the same.

Most American antiwar activists had bigger fish to fry in Syria at the time. And those who focused on Yemen had become obsessed with the drone war, which was new and controversial, though it had a relatively low impact. But beneath the radar, the Saudis had begun blockading and bombing the ports of an already malnourished country that must import 90 percent of its food.

Saudi warplanes bombed the bridges and roads. They bombed food processing plants and aid warehouses They bombed wedding parties and apartment buildings. And while the Obama administration curtailed arms exports to the Saudis, negotiated ceasefire agreements, and chastised Saudi forces in public, humanitarian organizations began to warn of a famine that could kill millions.

That was in the fall of 2016, when a Yemeni child was dying of hunger-related illness every 10 minutes or so. But as fall turned to winter and perhaps the most ignorant and callous president in American history entered office, the forced famine that had begun under a Saudi leadership, partially restrained by the Obama administration, descended into a hellish nightmare in which children were dying in the tens of thousands.

Now millions of lives were at risk in Yemen, as famines appeared in Somalia, South Sudan and northern Nigeria as well. Meanwhile, what a U.N. representative would dub "the worst humanitarian crisis since 1945" was just making its way to the back pages of the newspapers, as the drama of the Trump presidency took center stage. When Yemen finally did make the news, it was Trump's botched Navy SEAL operation that most interested the public – not the millions of civilians his administration was helping to starve.

While it has become quite common to refer to Stalin's forced famine of Ukraine in the early 1930s, and Mao's Great Famine of rural Chinese farmers in the late 1950s, as genocides, few if any have begun to speak of Yemen in such terms. Genocide is an expression that is not to be used in polite company – until the killings begin to taper off. Few people spoke of the Armenian genocide until late in the twentieth century, after all.[182] Israelis were even relatively quiet about the Holocaust until they found themselves lording it over others in 1967.[183] More recently in Syria, it was quite uncommon, among even activists supportive of the Syrian revolution, to hear Assad's war crimes referred to as genocide.

So whatever the nature of the crimes now being committed in Yemen, we should not expect to hear much talk of genocide for years to come. Nevertheless, the pattern of the bombings and their resultant starvation beg the question of whether America is now contributing to a genocide. And the pattern of bombings suggests that the Saudis are deliberately starving Yemenis into submission. One might excuse them for bombing the ports and bridges, but targeting aid warehouses is unusually extreme and blocking food imports is cruel and unnecessary.

There is little reason to believe the Saudis are deliberately attempting to kill off the Yemeni population, though. And if that is the case, then the forced famine in Yemen – like the Ukrainian Holodomor and Mao's Great Famine – should not technically be classified as a genocide. But with no expression to describe the deliberate murder of millions stronger than "crimes against humanity," which is ambiguous in both nature and scale, we should prepare for people to describe what is now happening in Yemen as a genocide. If that is the case, we should begin asking whether "the genocide in Yemen" will in the end turn out to be the great crime for which Trump is later remembered.

Given everything we know about President Trump, we cannot expect him to recognize that he may be a party to what is fast shaping up to be perhaps the most brutal genocide of this century. But as the haunting stick figures work their way into our moral imaginations and the death tolls climb higher, the story will break sooner or later. It is not possible to take part in a forced famine without restraint and not bear some responsibility for it, after all. And with all the best advisers, all the smartest people around you, there is no excuse for failing to grasp your own role as a mass murderer.

Righteous men have been going off in search of killers only to discover it was they themselves who committed the murder since at least as far back as Oedipus. Leadership is a lesson in self-discovery for even moral exemplars, but it is all the more so for the ignorant and righteous, who blame others while failing to look inside. Whether or not Trump is possessed of the moral development needed for such an inquiry, Americans themselves should begin to ask questions. In so doing, we may find that the phantom shadow of famine in Yemen points its ugly finger at our own callous ignorance. Somehow, we are able to focus on everything else under the sun but the most horrific crimes to which our nation has contributed in several decades. It is time to open our eyes and see.

THE CLIMATE WARS HAVE
BEGUN IN NIGERIA

If you want to understand why radical Islamists in northeastern Nigeria have been kidnapping little girls and massacring villagers, you would do well to look less to Islam and more to your own tailpipe instead. Boko Haram is largely a consequence of climate change, which has been drying out the African Sahel, the wide belt of grasslands south of the Sahara. But the processes of climate change tend to be slow and imperceptible, so we usually see only its symptoms, like some thief in the night who leaves only fingerprints, so we have failed to trace the Boko Haram connection.

Nigeria is a huge country, accounting for roughly a quarter the population of sub-Saharan Africa. And Boko Haram controls but a small portion of its northeast around Lake Chad. This once great lake in the heart of Africa supports the livelihoods of roughly 30 million people and provides water to about 68 million. Yet over the course of the last 40 years it has shrunk by roughly 90 percent. The United Nations Environment Program attributes about half of this decrease to patterns of grazing and overuse and the other half to climate change. This follows a more general pattern of regional desertification. According to the U.N., Nigeria loses 1,355 square miles of crop and rangeland to desertification each year. Population pressures diminish the size of already overworked farm plots, and this only compounds the climatic effects on the land.[184] The result is malnourishment for every other person in the northeastern state of Bornu.

The dry season there is a hunger season. With scant food and little rain to replenish crops, men tend to abandon their families and look elsewhere for work. Left to fend for themselves, the women often place their children under the care of religious teachers. And this is where recruitment for Boko Haram is intimately tied to desertification, suggests Greg Abolo, a Nigerian friend and public affairs analyst.

Abandoned children struggle with developing healthy attachments. Most become either too attached or too avoidant in their relationships. But religion is an extremely powerful source of group bonding, which ties people together through shared rituals and beliefs, and can therefore serve as a substitute family. This bonding through religion can come to the fore when environmental conditions disrupt settled ways of life. Add to this large numbers of unemployed young men, with little hope for the future, searching for a sense of connection and purpose, and the ground is laid for the cultish fanaticism of a quasi-religious movement like Boko Haram.

European slave traders and colonialists alike built an infrastructure best suited to siphoning off resources from interior Africa. Coupled with geographic differences, this has resulted in great inequalities within Nigeria. Whereas the south tends to be wealthy, the north tends to be poor. Whereas the south tends to be lush, the north tends to be arid. Whereas the south tends to be Christian, the north tends to be Muslim. And it is out of one of the poorest, driest, and most socially marginalized Muslim regions of the north that Boko Haram first grew into an insurgency in 2009. Since that time Boko Haram has, according to the Economist, killed some 16,000 people and displaced about a million.[185]

Nigeria consists of three main tribal groups, the Christian Igbos, the Muslim Hausa, and the mixed Yoruba. Most people vote along tribal lines, for ruling parties reward their fellow tribal members with jobs and other perks. This makes political campaigns a bit like intensive get-out-the-vote drives in which campaigning consists of a sort of rallying of troops. This can be destabilizing, especially in a country where democracy is not yet consolidated.

The balance of power among the tribes is a sensitive issue, for the system is highly prone to violence, suggests Prince Oluwatomisin Oyetunji. Using the full force of military might against Boko Haram thus runs the risk of strengthening the rebellion. It is a danger American troops have all too often confronted in their own war on terror. And yet, the inability of the much larger Nigerian army to defeat this small insurgency has resulted in finger pointing all around.

Boko Haram has its origins not in the larger Muslim Hausa tribe, but rather the much smaller Kanuri tribe, which has long been centered around Lake Chad. The tribe consists of the remnants of a pre-colonial empire that has long resisted outside influence. While the world outside Nigeria may view Boko Haram as an Islamic problem, a closer look reveals environmental stresses, contributing to poverty and inequality for the members of this and other marginalized tribes.

The insurgency is symptomatic of more endemic problems, and addressing these will require more than military might. Nigeria needs to devote more resources to poverty alleviation. But freeing up these resources may require purging the system of tribalism, which tends to result in passing wealth to the most powerful tribes. Economic development can make this easier, for it makes it possible to pay higher wages to civil servants who might otherwise be tempted to corruption. And it would free up tax dollars for building a stronger social safety net. But if Nigeria is to develop in such a healthy direction, it will need to be the right kind of development. Recent years have seen most economic growth tied to oil extraction, which is unsustainable in the long run and tends to be siphoned off into the hands of ever-more powerful elites. Nigeria also needs to fight desertification, and it can do this through soil conservation, better grazing practices, and widespread reforestation.

The climate wars have already begun in Nigeria. It is a state burdened with poverty, corruption, tribalism and desertification. It is out of this milieu that Boko Haram has arisen. But Nigeria has many strengths through which this militant movement might be overcome. Nigeria is in the midst of a democratic and economic transition. And it sometimes seems as if Nigerians themselves are experiencing a literary and spiritual renaissance. Nigerians can be strikingly optimistic and intelligent. And they are making use of their increasing levels of education and access to social media to re-envision their futures. Boko Haram is but a small part of this much greater country that is gradually awakening. Perhaps we should focus less on the tired old theme of militant Islam and more on the social and environmental inequalities out of which they have arisen. Then we might apply Nigeria's strengths to overcoming its weaknesses.

THE ONLY WAY TO
OVERCOME GENOCIDE

When the U.S. was invading Iraq back in 1991, I was just starting college. Frustrated with the wartime chauvinism, I made up a peace poster, walked to the highest hill in the center of the quad and tied it in the ground, and sat out the war, as protesters gathered around. A fellow protest leader, who later became my best friend, told me about a pro-war politician who was holding a Town Hall meeting. So, we went to debate him and it turned out to be Newt Gingrich, the soon-to-be brains behind the Republican takeover of Congress in 1994. But he turned out to be an empty legend. Somehow, two freshman college students were able to go head-to-head with him, on his home turf on the border of Alabama, for roughly an hour, with simple moral arguments, as the tiny small-town audience watched in silence.

Still, however many marches we held, and however many holes we pricked in the hypocritical logic of American imperialism, it did not stop the Iraqi army from being slaughtered en masse, as they limped back from Kuwait. After killing the better part of Saddam's defenseless and retreating army, President Bush Sr. suggested that it might be a good time for the Shiites and Kurds to rebel. An Iraqi friend, Maithem Salih, told me how the young men of his city responded to the call, bravely taking up their rusty old Kalashnikovs before being promptly mowed down by Saddam's modern army.

With eyes wide and body stiff, he spoke of how he took refuge with his mom in an ancient mosque. They could not imagine Saddam's troops firing on the monument, but when the tanks came, the troops bombed the great gate, behind which thousands had gathered, firing into the densest parts of the crowd. Saddam would later slaughter all the young men who had risen up, burying them in mass graves that would not be uncovered until over a decade later. What Saddam did return to families at the time were mere body parts, according to Salih, crudely assembled in bloody bags. It was all part of his regime of terror.

America has taken a lot of blame recently for causing the rise of Isis. America destabilized Iraq and opened a vacuum into which sprang a multitude of militias. Saddam may have been a brutal dictator but it is argued that the chaos of civil war and Isis is worse. Whether this is true or false, the conditions leading to the rise of Isis run much deeper than American involvement.

Upon entering office through a coup in 1979, Saddam quickly launched a territorial war with Iran. It was largely trench warfare and it left about a million dead. The loyalty of the ethnic Kurds soon came into question, as their population straddled the border between Iran and Iraq. So, Saddam began to kill off their men of fighting age. He used chemical weapons against villages and pushed survivors into the cities.[186] And while America was his ally at the beginning of this genocidal campaign, eventually he was sanctioned.[187]

This sort of history can leave a people severely traumatized. Much like Isis, Saddam used beheadings to terrorize his victims; and like Isis, his brutality was stunning and blunt. Both Saddam and Isis were Sunnis, who comprise about 20 percent of the Iraqi population. The Sunnis were hit hardest by the American invasion in 2003. And for this reason, many of Saddam's supporters and even some of his former Generals have made common cause with Isis. Isis began its life as a series of militias, following the American invasion in 2003. But they came to strength through the civil war in Syria. The Assad regime in Syria has itself engaged in the starvation of whole cities and the widespread torture of prisoners of war. Much of the brutality of Isis originated in the fight against Assad as well. The war victimized Isis fighters, and many are seeking to exact revenge.[188]

All of this suggests that what we are seeing now is a repetition of some of the terror inflicted under Saddam and Assad. Terror is often repeated throughout history because it is so traumatizing. The mind has a tendency to fixate on traumatic events, the bombing of one's home or the sight of a father's severed head. People who are victimized come to see the world in terms of victims and perpetrators, so trauma victims often exchange roles with their perpetrators over time.

The collective traumas that are now being unleashed in Iraq spring from multiple sources. They are held within the bodies of ordinary Iraqis and embodied in tribal codes of conduct. My Iraqi friend suggests that the only way to overcome the fighting that is now occurring between Sunnis and Shias is through generations of secular peace – but getting there is the hard part.

After reconnecting with my best friend from college, two decades later, we recalled our own efforts to promote peace. Perhaps the most absurd memory from our days of protesting was a poster we created for one of our demonstrations. "Take Off Your Body Condom and Impregnate the World With Love." The poster embodied all of the freedom, safety, and privilege that made us believe it possible to achieve a world without war. And it pointed to the very real relationship between the armored tank and the armored body. Peace in the Middle East will be difficult to achieve until ordinary people release their deepest traumas, which are largely held in the body. But the whirlwind of violence that is now sweeping through the region will require solutions that surpass even the most sober of slogans.

We would all do well to let ourselves sink a little more deeply into the historical traumas of ordinary Iraqis before offering our own opinions as to what should be done. And we would all do well to let go of the traumas we are holding in our own emotional-bodies. Watching traumas unfold from the outside can itself be traumatizing. But it can also lead us to open to the suffering of others, and through opening to the worst humanity has to offer, to lift ourselves up to a higher vision.

Yet, the higher vision is often much closer to home than we might believe. This was vividly illustrated to me by a Bosnian Muslim soldier in Sarajevo, who spent his youth fighting the Serbian Orthodox Christian soldiers with whom he now shared a military unit. In broken English, he suggested it was as if the war had never happened, that they were now like family. The Muslim victims of ethnic cleansing and genocide, whose wives and sisters had been gang raped by Serbian soldiers in an effort to impregnate them and put an end to their race, now worked hand in glove with the very perpetrators of those same crimes. And not only that, the military they shared was the most integrated institution in the country, made possible by substantial NATO involvement. As if to drive the point home, the friend from whom he broke off conversation to convey this Bosnian commonplace was none other than a greying Serbian soldier, just about the right age to have been a perpetrator of those very same crimes against humanity suffered by friends and family. They were brothers in arms, but brothers from opposite lines of one of the most genocidal battles of the late twentieth century.

The same human family that might kill itself off can also live not only in peace and harmony but working together in cooperation and beauty. It is a vision that is often hard to sustain amid the brutalities of war; but in learning to find a path to cooperation, amid the memories of genocide and the traumas it evokes, it can sometimes seem as if anything is possible. Perhaps genocide will be overcome the same way humanity has overcome all the slings and arrows of outrageous fortune, strewn through its course on down through the millennia. Perhaps we will muddle through, perhaps we will rise to the occasion, looking the killers in the eyes and acting to stop it; and perhaps genocide is just the odd note of dissonance amid a far more lofty score, working out the contradictions of an imperfect animal, a little smarter than the apes, and yet not so perfect as the better angels of our imagination.

THE MOST DANGEROUS YEAR SINCE 1941

We are now living in the most dangerous year since at least 1941, when the Third Reich was at the height of its power and fascism threatened to engulf the world. There are arguably more famines raging in the world today than at any time in generations, more failed states than at any time since the dissolution of the British and French empires, more groups committing genocide than at any time since the Second World War. But these troubles are merely symptomatic of deeper disorders and dwarfed by more global threats.

The two countries most capable of annihilating the planet through nuclear war are arguably led by more aggressive and callous leaders than at any time since the death of Stalin. Rightwing nationalists, fascists, and authoritarians now head the greater portion of the world's major states. The number of democratic states is in decline, with significant deterioration of democratic institutions in even the most well-established democracies.[189] And the world order itself is fast becoming anarchic, dysfunctional, and prone to conflict.

Whereas famine is absent from the world in most years, with the last declared in Somalia in 2011, there are now 20 million people at risk of starvation in South Sudan, Northeastern Nigeria, Yemen, and Somalia. The famines now raging in these places have been described by a senior U.N. official as "the worst humanitarian crisis since 1945." And whereas in most years, the world might band together to mitigate their worst damage, these have gone virtually unnoticed and have been largely ignored.

Most of these countries tend to top the listings of fragile states, and the number of fragile states has been growing for the past decade.[190] Fragile states tend to bleed refugees, terrorists, trafficked humans, and illegal drugs, and they are often wracked with conflict. The conflicts in Nigeria, South Sudan, and Somalia have made it difficult to farm and provide food aid, but the famine in Yemen has been largely manufactured through the deliberate bombing and blockading of ports and the obliteration of vital infrastructure.

Whereas scarcely a year goes by without some place in the world experiencing a level of mass murder approaching genocide, seldom are more than a couple of states engaged in such killings. And it is rare for large coalitions to engage in such killing together. But multiple states are arguably committing genocide against the rebel opposition in Syria; and at least a dozen states, including the U.S. and U.K., are backing the Saudis forced starvation of Yemen. Meanwhile, Isis is carrying out a genocide of Yezidis and Burma against its minority Rohingya.

The challenges are interlinked. As the world order breaks down, nations retreat in the face of a more frightening world, and as nations retreat, the world becomes more frightening. State failure and genocide spur refugee flows, which lead developed nations to retreat in fear, and as developed nations retreat in fear, state failure and genocide carry on unchecked. This is but another face of collective trauma, only this time played out on the global stage.

Whereas the world order has been largely stable since the Second World War, overseen by an array of multilateral organizations, which are themselves overseen by a couple dozen or so developed democracies, the rise of rightwing nationalist and fascist governments in most major states threatens to smash that order to bits. Rightwing nationalists now head the U.S. and U.K., China and India, Russia and Turkey, Egypt and Saudi Arabia, Poland and Hungary. Together they threaten to make global concerted action a thing of the past. All of this is complicated by democratic decline.

Whereas the number of democratic states has been rising now for hundreds of years, with brief declines in stair-step fashion, it has been declining for roughly a decade and this may be the worst year yet. It is not simply that dictators have gotten better at maintaining power, citizens in states as varied as the Philippines and Egypt, America and Russia, are clambering for strong men under whose authority they might submit. And this has brought to power more dangerous leaders.

Whereas the two most heavily armed nuclear states have long been careful to avoid a nuclear showdown, with even most Soviet leaders since Stalin working for peace, the U.S. has just elected a potentially sociopathic and erratic leader in favor of their use, while Russia's leader may be the most belligerent in the world today. With the global order in flux, and both leaders bolstered by tough images and talk, the potential for nuclear holocaust may never have been greater.

We cannot afford to panic right now, because panicking fuels the contraction into rightwing nationalism, which pits everyone against each other. But we need to recognize the crisis we are in and that will mean a whole lot of panicking. It is a challenge common to every organization and human system in decline – panic but don't panic – but this time it is the world system that is in rapid dissolution. This may actually be the most dangerous year ever the history of human civilization.

Whereas the Third Reich threatened to sweep the world in 1941, today we can destroy the planet in an instant. Meanwhile, the global climate system is beginning to spiral out of control, and the global turn toward nationalism means climate change will get even less attention. Meanwhile nationalist governments will likely adopt pro-natalist programs, as they so often do, and this will intensify population stresses over time.

However, the greatest danger is not so much a nuclear Trump administration or even a rapid escalation of multiple global wars, but rather the vicious circle of unmet global challenges fueling a retreat into nationalism, which is all the worse for the failure of nationalist governments to take on the challenge of managing a deteriorating global order. If this is the case, then 2017 might mark the beginning of the end of human civilization.

And yet, until half a decade or so ago, the future was looking quite bright. World hunger was on the decline. Mortality rates were declining the world over. The Arab Spring and mass protest movements in India and Brazil, Ukraine and Turkey, promised yet another wave of democratization. More children were being educated and vaccinated the world over – even in failed states.[191] It is quite possible some of these trends will continue amid a general degeneration of the global order. It is quite possible the world is experiencing merely the instability that so often accompanies development to a higher level of integrated complexity.

We simply do not know how long the fascist moment will last. We do not know if it has already reached its high water mark or if the worst is yet to come. We do not know whether it is suggestive of a temporary backlash or a more long term trend. And we do not know whether or not the same forces that brought it into being will undo it just as fast.

Rightwing nationalists have been brought to power by the forces of globalization, mass inequality, technological complexity, a generational backlash, and social media. But each of these forces might just as well have brought about its opposite. Over the course of the twenty-first century, we should expect ever cheaper and faster transportation, easier money transfers, increasing immigration, more technological interconnectivity, stronger global networks, and more interconnected global environmental challenges, whoever is in charge. Hence, those who would wish globalization away will ultimately fail. Similarly, mass inequality is only likely to grow with increasing automation and globalization. And it will be felt ever more strongly as we are exposed to ever more people on the other side of the planet. But the rightwing nationalists have no solutions to inequality either; nor are they likely to turn back the clock on technological development.

The same forces that brought rightwing nationalists to power can just as easily take them out. It is just as easy for liberals to organize on social media as it is for conservatives. For awhile it looked like social media would bring about another wave of democratization. Meanwhile, the generational backlash among Baby Boomers will be weakened with each passing year, as Millennials come to assume power and an older generation tires of pushing the river.

Nothing short of the fate of the world hangs in the balance between these two great global forces. Hence, 2017 may not only be the most dangerous year in the history of the world but the most pivotal as well. The outcome of this epic struggle is largely in our own hands, and the way we respond will have a lot to do with the way we choose to face collective trauma. We can embrace it with empathy and equanimity, facing up to its impacts with relaxed bodies and minds, forgiving its perpetrators for their transgressions, while working for justice. Or else, we can retreat from it in fear and denial, thereby fueling the rightwing backlash and the cycle of violence.

It is a truly momentous choice for a decisive moment in history.

If this book has instilled anything in its readers it should be a felt sense of the traumas animating the deterioration of the global order. The aftermath of countless collective traumas has resulted in a world of peoples retreating in fear. People will continue to fight, and they will continue to die as all humans must, sometimes lost and lonely, and sometimes in droves. But we can minimize the violence and soften the blows. If this book inspires the action needed to save but a single life it will have accomplished its purpose. But when many millions are at risk in holocausts like the famines in Yemen and Nigeria, and virtually nothing is being written about them, each of us can alter the course of history by simply facing up to these tragedies with sustained attention and care.

Theo Horesh
Oxford, United Kingdom

BIBLIOGRAPHY

BOOKS

Acikyildiz, Birgūl. *The Yezidis: The History of a Community, Culture, and Religion.* I.B. Taurus. 2014.

Appiah, Kwame Anthony. *The Honor Code: How Moral Revolutions Happen.* W.W. Norton and Company. 2011.

Arendt, Hannah. *The Origins of Totalitarianism.* Schocken. 1951.

Arendt, Hannah. *Eichmann in Jerusalem: A Report on the Banality of Evil.* Viking. 1968.

Armitage, David. *The Declaration of Independence: A Global History.* Harvard University Press. 2008.

Armstrong, Karen. *Fields of Blood: Religion and the History of Violence.* Anchor. 2015.

Aslan, Reza. *Zealot: The Life and Times of Jesus of Nazareth.* Random House. 2013.

Atzmon, Gilad. *The Wandering Who? A Study of Jewish Identity Politics.* Zero Books. 2011.

Barghouti, Mourid. *I Saw Ramallah.* Anchor. 2003.

Becker, Ernest. *The Denial of Death.* Free Press. 1997.

Beinhart, Peter. *The Crisis of Zionism.* Picador. 2013.

Ben-Ami, Shlomo. *Scars of War, Wounds of Peace: The Israeli-Arab Tragedy.* Oxford University Press. 2007.

Bengsston, Jesper. *Struggle for Freedom: Aung San Suu Kyi.* Fourth Estate. 2011.

Berne M.D., Eric. *Games People Play: The Basic Handbook of Transactional Analysis.* Grove Press. 1981.

Bird, Christiane. *A Thousand Sighs, A Thousand Revolts: Journeys in Kurdistan.* Ballantine Books. 2004.

Blanford, Nicholas. *Warriors of God: Inside Hezbollah's Thirty-Year Struggle Against Israel.* Random House. 2011.

Bloxham, Donald. *The Great Game of Genocide: Imperialism, Nationalism, and the Destruction of the Ottoman Armenians.* Oxford University Press. 2007.

Borg, Marcus. *The Last Week: What the Gospels Really Teach About Jesus's Final Days in Jerusalem.* Harper One. 2007.

Borri, Francesca. *Syrian Dust: Reporting from the Heart of the War.* Seven Stories Press. 2016.

Bowen, Murray. *Family Therapy in Clinical Practice.* Jason Aronson Inc. 1978.

Braley, Alia. *A Nonviolent Grassroots Response to the Islamic State: Strategic Analysis.* Harvard University Masters Thesis. 2015.

Bremmer, Ian. *Every Nation for Itself: What Happens When No One Leads the World.* Portfolio. 2013.

Bregman, Ahron, *Cursed Victory: A History of Israel and the Occupied Territories, 1967 to Present.* Pegasus Books. 2015.

Browning, Christopher R. *Ordinary Men: Reserve Police Battalion 101 and the Final Solution in Poland.* Harper Perennial. 1998.

Buber, Martin. *A Land of Two Peoples: Martin Buber on Jews and Arabs.* University of Chicago Press. 2005.

Carter, Jimmy. *Palestine: Peace Not Apartheid.* Simon and Schuster. 2007.

Chenoweth, Erica and Stephan, Maria. *Why Civil Resistance Works: The Strategic Logic of Nonviolent Conflict.* Columbia University Press. 2012.

Chomsky, Noam. *The Fateful Triangle: The United States, Israel, and the Palestinians.* South End Press. 1999.

Clark, Victoria. *Yemen: Dancing on the Heads of Snakes.* Yale University Press. 2010.

Collier, Paul. *The Bottom Billion: Why the Poorest Countries are Failing and What Can Be Done About It.* Oxford University Press. 2007.

Conway, Gordon. *One Billion Hungry: Can We Feed the World?* Comstock Publishing Associates. 2012.

Cook, Jonathan. *Disappearing Palestine: Israel's Experiment's in Human Despair.* Zed Books. 2008.

Crossan, John Dominic. *The Historical Jesus: The Life of a Mediterranean Jewish Peasant.* Harper One. 1993.

De Waal, Thomas. *The Great Catastrophe: Armenians and Turks in the Shadow of Genocide.* Oxford University Press. 2015.

Deutscher, Isaac. *The Non-Jewish Jew and Other Essays.* OUP. 1968.

Dikotter, Frank. *Mao's Great Famine: The History of China's Most Devastating Catastrophe, 1958-1962.* Walker Books. 2011.

Doyle, Sir Arthur Conan. *The Memoirs of Sherlock Holmes.* The Strand. 1893.

Foucault, Michel. *Discipline and Punish: The Birth of the Prison.* Vintage Books. 1995.

Finkelstein, Norman G. *Beyond Chutzpah: On the Misuse of Anti-Semitism and the Abuse of History.* University of California Press. 2008.

Finkelstein, Norman G. *The Holocaust Industry: Reflections on the Exploitation of Jewish Suffering.* Verso. 2015.

Freud, Sigmund. *Moses and Monotheism.* Alfred and Knopf. 1939.

Freud, Sigmund. *Beyond the Pleasure Principle.* W.W. Norton and Company. 1990.

Fromm, Erich. *Escape from Freedom.* Farrar and Reinhart. 1941.

Glenny, Misha. *The Fall of Yugoslavia: The Third Balkan War.* Penguin Books. 1996.

Goldhagen, Daniel Jonah. *Hitler's Willing Executioners: Ordinary Germans and the Holocaust.* Vintage. 1997.

Goldhagen, Daniel. *Worse Than War: Genocide, Eliminationism, and the Ongoing Assault on Humanity.* Public Affairs. 2009.

Gordon, Neve. *Israel's Occupation.* University of California Press. 2008.

Gorenberg, Gershom. *The Unmaking of Israel.* Harper Perennial. 2012.

Grossman, David. *The Yellow Wind.* Picador. 2002.

Grossman, David. *To the End of the Land.* Vintage. 2011.

Haas, Richard. *World in Disarray: American Foreign Policy and the Crisis of the Old Order.* Penguin Press. 2017.

Hall, Brian. *The Impossible Country: A Journey Through the last Days of Yugoslavia.* Penguin Books. 1995.

Hatzfeld, Jean. *Machete Season: The Killers in Rwanda Speak.* Picador. 2006.

Herman, Judith. *Trauma and Recovery: The Aftermath of Abuse – From Domestic Abuse to Political Terror.* Basic Books. 2015.

Hever, Shir. *The Political Economy of Israel's Occupation: Repression Beyond Exploitation.* Pluto Press. 2010.

Hokayem, Emile. *Syria's Uprising and the Fracturing of the Levant.* Routledge. 2013.

Holbrooke, Richard. *To End a War.* Modern Library. 1999.

Horesh, Theo. *Convergence: The Globalization of Mind.* Bauu Institute. 2014.

Hourani, Albert. *Arabic Thought in the Liberal Age 1798-1939.* Cambridge University Press. 1983.

Hourani, Albert. *A History of the Arab Peoples.* Belknap Press of Harvard University Press. 1991.

Ibrahim, Azeem. *The Rohingyas: Inside Myanmar's Hidden Genocide.* Hurst. 2016.

Johnson, Gregory D. *The Last Refuge: Yemen, Al-Qaeda, and America's War in Arabia.* W.W. Norton and Company. 2014.

Judah, Tim. *The Serbs: History, Myth and the Destruction of Yugoslavia.* Yale

University Press. 2010.

Kalyvas, Stathis. *Modern Greece: What Everyone Needs to Know.* Oxford University Press. 2015.

Kassab, Robin Yassin and Al-Shami, Leila. *Burning Country: Syrians in Revolution and War.* Pluto Press. 2016.

Kenny, Charles. *Getting Better: Why Global Development is Succeeding – and How We Can Improve the World Even More.* Basic Books. 2012.

Khalidi, Rashid. *The Iron Cage: The Story of the Palestinian Struggle for Statehood.* Beacon Press. 2007.

Kimmerling, Baruch and Migdal, Joel S. *The Palestinian People: A History.* Harvard University Press. 2003.

Kimmerling, Baruch. *The Invention and Decline of Israeliness: State, Society, and Military.* University of California Press. 2005.

King, Mary Elizabeth. *A Quiet Revolution: The First Palestinian Intifada and Nonviolent Resistance.* Nation Books. 2007.

Kissinger, Henry. *World Order.* Penguin Books. 2015.

Lackner, Helen. *Why Yemen Matters: A Society in Transition.* Saqi Books. 2014.

Lakoff, George. *Metaphors We Live By.* University of Chicago Press. 2003.

Larkin, Emma. *Finding George Orwell in Burma.* Penguin Books. 2006.

Lawrence, Quil. *Invisible Nation: How the Kurds Quest for Statehood is Shaping Iraq and the Middle East.* Walker Books. 2008.

Lemarchand, Réne. *The Dynamics of Violence in Central Africa.* University of Pennsylvania Press. 2007.

Levine, Amy-Jill. *The Misunderstood Jew: The Church and the Scandal of the Jewish Jesus.* Harper One. 2007.

Levine, Peter A. *Waking the Tiger: Healing Trauma.* North Atlantic Books. 1997.

Lewis, Bernard. *The Jews of Islam.* Princeton University Press. 2014.

Lindsay, Brendan C. *Murder State: California's Native American Genocide 1846-1873.* University of Nebraska Press. 2013.

Little, Jonathan and Mandell, Charlotte. *Syrian Notebooks: Inside the Homs Uprising.* Verso. 2015.

Madley, Benjamin. *An American Genocide: The United States and the California Indian Tragedy 1846-1873.* Yale University Press. 2016.

Makdisi, Saree. *Palestine Inside Out: An Everyday Occupation.* W.W. Norton and Company. 2010.

Malthus, Thomas Robert. *An Essay on the Principles of Population As It Affects the Future Improvements of Society.* J. Johnson in St. Paul's Church Yard. 1798.

Mansfield, Stephen. *The Miracle of the Kurds: A Remarkable Story of Hope*

Reborn in Northern Iraq. Worthy Publishing. 2014.

Marshall McLuhan. *Understanding Media: The Extensions of Man.* McGraw-Hill. 1964.

Mazower, Mark. *Salonica, City of Ghosts: Muslims and Jews 1430-1950.* Vintage. 2006.

Mearsheimer, John J. *The Tragedy of Great Power Politics.* W.W. Norton and Company. 2014.

Morris, Benny. *One State, Two States.* Yale University Press. 2010.

Morris, Benny. *Righteous Victims: A History of the Zionist-Arab Conflict, 1881-2001.* Vintage. 2001.

Myint-U, Thant. *The Making of Modern Burma.* Cambridge University Press. 2001.

Norenzayan, Ara. *Big Gods: How Religion Transformed Cooperation and Conflict.* Princeton University Press. 2015.

Norton, Augustus Richard. *Hezbollah: A Short History.* Princeton University Press. 2014.

Nozick, Robert. *Anarchy, State, and Utopia.* Basic Books. 1974.

Nusseibeh, Sari. *Once Upon a Country.* Picador. 2008.

Nusseibeh, Sari. *What is a Palestinian State Worth?* Harvard University Press. 2013.

Olussoga, David and Erichsen, Casper W. *The Kaiser's Holocaust: Germany's Forgotten Genocide and the Colonial Roots of Nazism.* Faber and Faber. 2011.

Oz, Amos. *In the Land of Israel.* Mariner Books. 1993.

Oz, Amos. *A Tale of Love and Darkness.* Mariner Books. 2005.

Pappé, Ilan. *The Ethnic Cleansing of Palestine.* Oneworld Publications. 2007.

Paarlberg, Robert. *Starved for Science: How Biotechnology is Being Kept Out of Africa.* Harvard University Press. 2009.

Pamuk, Orhan. *Istanbul: Memories and the City.* 2006.

Pinker, Steven. *The Better Angels of Our Nature: Why Violence Declines.* Penguin Books. 2012.

Pound, Ezra trans. *Confucius: The Unwobbling Pivot. The Great Digest. The Analects.* New Directions. 1969.

Prunier, Gerard. *Africa's World War: Congo, the Rwandan Genocide, and the Making of a Continental Catastrophe.* Oxford University Press. 2011.

Power, Samantha. *A Problem from Hell: America and the Age of Genocide.* Basic Books. 2013.

Purdue, Theda and Green, Michael. *The Cherokee Nation and the Trail of Tears.* Penguin Books. 2008.

Rose, Jacqueline. *The Last Resistance.* Verso. 2013.

Russel, Gerard. *Heirs to Forgotten Kingdoms: Journeys Into the Disappearing Religions of the Middle East.* Basic Books. 2015.

Saleh, Yassin Al-Haj. *Impossible Revolution: Making Sense of the Syrian Tragedy.* Haymarket Books. 2017.

Salibi, Kamal. *A House of Many Mansions: The History of Lebanon Reconsidered.* University of California Press. 1990.

Sand, Shlomo. *The Invention of the Jewish People.* Verso. 2010.

Sartre, Jean Paul. *Anti-Semite and Jew.* Schocken Books. 1948.

Segev, Tom. *The Seventh Million: Israelis and the Holocaust.* Picador. 2000.

Sen, Amartya. *Development as Freedom.* Anchor. 2000.

Sharpe, Gene and Paulson, Joshua. *Waging Nonviolent Struggle: 20th Century Practice and 21st Century Potential.* Porter Sargent Pub. 2005.

Shavit, Ari. *My Promised Land: The Triumph and Tragedy of Israel.* Spiegel and Grau. 2015.

Shehadeh, Raja. *Strangers in the House: Coming of Age in Occupied Palestine.* Penguin Books. 2003.

Silberman, Neil Asher and Finkelstein, Israel. *The Bible Unearthed: Archeology's New Vision of Ancient Israel and the Origins of Its Sacred Scriptures.* Touchstone. 2002.

Smith, Anthony D. *Nations and Nationalism in a Global Era.* Polity. 1995.

Stearns, Jason. *Dancing in the Glory of Monsters: The Collapse of the Congo and the Great War of Africa.* Public Affairs. 2012.

Tilley, Virginia. *The One-State Solution: A Breakthrough for Peace in the Israeli-Palestinian Deadlock.* University of Michigan Press. 2010.

Van Dam, Nikolaos. *The Struggle for Power in Syria: Politics and Society Under Assad and the Ba'ath Party.* I.B. Tauris. 2011.

Van Der Kolk, Bessel. *The Body Keeps the Score: Brain, Mind, and Body in the Healing of Trauma.* Viking Press. 2014.

Victoria, Brian Daizen. *Zen at War.* Rowman and Littlefield Publishers. 2006.

Voltaire. *Candide, or Optimism.* 1759.

Weiss, Michael and Hassan, Hassan. *ISIS: Inside the Army of Terror.* Regan Arts. 2015.

Weizman, Eyal. *Hollow Land: Israel's Architecture of Occupation.* Verso. 2017.

Young, Michael. *The Ghosts of Martyrs Square: An Eyewitness Account of Lebanon's Life Struggle.* Simon and Schuster. 2014.

ARTICLES

Adalah: The Legal Center for Arab Minority Rights in Israel. *Discriminatory Laws in Israel.* 2016.

Adalah: The Legal Center for Arab Minority Rights in Israel. *Discrimination in land and housing against Palestinian citizens in Israel in 2015.* March 2016.

Agence France-Presse. *"Era of Propaganda:" Press Freedom in Decline, Says Reporters Without Borders.* The Guardian. April 2016.

Akiva, Eldar. *Netanyahu Has Rejected Two-State Solution.* Al-Monitor. February 2015.

Amnesty International. *Discrimination of Palestinians Within Israel.* May 2013.

Amnesty International. *Israel/Gaza Conflict. Questions and Answers.* July 2014.

Amnesty International. *Myanmar: Crimes Against Humanity Terrorize and Drive Rohingya Out.* October 2017.

BBC. *Gaza Crisis: Toll of Operations.* September 2014.

Bailey, Sarah Pulliam. *American Evangelicals' Support for Israel is Waning, Reports Say.* Huffington Post. April 2014.

Brannon, Susan. *Hebron Settlers.* The Electronic Intifada. July 2002.

Carter, Jimmy. *A Five-Nation Plan to End the Syrian Crisis.* New York Times. October 2015.

Chelala, Cesar. *Destroying Palestinian Olive Trees.* The Globalist. November 2010.

Chulov, Martin. *Besieged and Terrified, and the Food is About to Run Out for Damascus Refugees.* The Guardian. April 2014.

Coursen-Neff, Zama. *Discrimination Against Palestinian Arab Children in the Israeli Education System.* International Law and Politics. Volume 36: 749.

Daher, Aurélie. *Hezbollah and the Syria Conflict.* The Middle East Institute. November 2015.

Foreign Policy. *Fragile States Index.* 2015.

Freedman, David H. *The Truth About Genetically Modified Food.* September 2013. Scientific American.

Freedom House. *Freedom in the World 2017: Freedom Decline Continues Amid Rising Populism and Autocracy.* January 2017.

Ghattas, Kim. *Syrian Torture: Will Photos Turn US Opinion.* BBC News. January 2015.

Ghattas, Kim. *US Policy on Syria "Depends on Success in Libya."* The Guardian. May 2011.

Haas, Amira. *Palestinian Jerusalemites Go Work Abroad and Get Residency*

Revoked Upon Return. Haaretz. June 2010.

Hasan, Mehdi. *The Palestinians of Yarmouk and the Shameful Silence When Israel is Not to Blame.* The Guardian. April 2015.

Hubbard, Ben and Kirkpatrick, David. *Photo Archive is Said to Show Widespread Torture in Syria.* New York Times. January 2014.

Human Rights Watch. *Soldier's Punishment for Using Boy as "Human Shield" Inadequate.* November 2010.

Human Rights Watch. *All You Can Do is Pray: Crimes Against Humanity and Ethnic Cleansing of Rohingya Muslims in Burma's Arakan State.* April 2013.

Human Rights Watch. *Israel: Security Forces Abuse Palestinian Children.* July 2015.

Human Rights Watch. *Rohingya Crisis.* October 2017.

Isaac, Jad. *The Role of Groundwater in the Water Conflict and Resolution Between Israelis and Palestinians.* International Symposium on Groundwater Sustainability. Applied Research Institute Jerusalem.

Israeli Committee on House Demolitions. *Comprehensive Briefing on Home Demolitions.* December 2017.

Kerry, John F. *Assad's War of Starvation.* Foreign Policy. October 2013.

Marsh, Katherine and Tisdall, Simon. *Syrian Troops Shoot Dead Protesters in Days of Turmoil.* The Guardian. April 2011.

Martinez, Michael. *Is Hamas Using Human Shields in Gaza? The Answer is Complicated.* CNN. July 2014.

McGreal, Chris. *World Court Tells Israel to Tear Down Illegal Wall.* The Guardian. July 10, 2004.

New Israel Fund. *Arab Sector: NIF Grantees Fight Discrimination in Arab Education.* December 2005.

Rafizadeh, Majid. *Iran's Forces Outnumber Assad's in Syria.* The Gatestone Institute International Policy Council. November 2016.

Ramahi, Sawsen. *Israel is Stealing Palestinian and Arab Water.* Middle East Monitor. May 2014.

Rotman, David. *Why We Will Need Genetically Modified Foods.* December 2013. MIT Technology Review.

Sasson, Talya. *Summary of the Opinion Concerning Unauthorized Outposts.* Israel Ministry of Foreign Affairs. March 2005.

Saleh, Yassin Al Haj. *Assad's Killing Industry and the Role of Intellectuals.* Al-Jumhuriya. March 2014.

Shuttlesworth, Kate. *For Arabs in Israel, Curriculum Choice is Politically Charged.* New York Times. January 2014.

Slackman, Michael. *Syrian Leader Blames "Conspiracy" for Turmoil.* New York Times. March 2011.

Stewart, Phil and Strobel, Warren. *U.S. to Halt Some Arms Sales to Saudis, Citing Civilian Deaths in Yemen Campaign.* Reuters. December 2016.

The Economist. *Nigeria and Boko Haram: The Black Flag in Africa.* January 2015.

United Nations Children's Fund. *Children in Israeli Military Detention.* February 2013.

United Nations Children's Fund. *Malnutrition Amongst Children in Yemen at an All-Time High.* December 2016.

United Nations Economic and Social Council: Economic Commission for Africa. *Africa Review Report on Drought and Desertification.* October 2007.

United Nations Office for the Coordination of Humanitarian Affairs. *Yemen: A Child Under the Age of Five Dies Every 10 Minutes of Preventable Causes – UN Humanitarian Chief.* January 2017.

Zonszein, Mairav. *Israel killed More Palestinian in 2014 Than in Any Other Year Since 1967.* The Guardian. March 2015.

ENDNOTES

1   Browning, Christopher R. *Ordinary Men: Reserve Police Battalion 101 and the Final Solution in Poland.* Harper Perennial. 1998. Goldhagen, Daniel Jonah. *Hitler's Willing Executioners: Ordinary Germans and the Holocaust.* Vintage. 1997.

2   Armitage, David. *The Declaration of Independence: A Global History.* Harvard University Press. 2008.

3   Herman, Judith. *Trauma and Recovery: The Aftermath of Abuse – From Domestic Abuse to Political Terror.* Basic Books. 2015.

4   Bessel Van Der Kolk. *The Body Keeps the Score: Brain, Mind, and Body in the Healing of Trauma.* Viking Press. 2014.

5   Becker, Ernest. *The Denial of Death.* Free Press. 1997.

6   Pappé, Ilan. *The Ethnic Cleansing of Palestine.* Oneworld Publications. 2007. Khalidi, Rashid. *The Iron Cage: The Story of the Palestinian Struggle for Statehood.* Beacon Press. 2007. Kimmerling, Baruch and Migdal, Joel S. *The Palestinian People: A History.* Harvard University Press. 2003. Morris, Benny. *Righteous Victims: A History of the Zionist-Arab Conflict, 1881-2001.* Vintage. 2001.

7   Herman, Judith. *Trauma and Recovery: The Aftermath of Abuse – From Domestic Abuse to Political Terror.* Basic Books. 2015.

8   Bessel Van Der Kolk. *The Body Keeps the Score: Brain, Mind, and Body in the Healing of Trauma.* Viking Press. 2014.

9   Purdue, Theda and Green, Michael. *The Cherokee Nation and the Trail of Tears.* Penguin Books. 2008.

10   Lindsay, Brendan C. *Murder State: California's Native American Genocide 1846-1873.* University of Nebraska Press. 2013. Madley, Benjamin. *An American Genocide: The United States and the California Indian Tragedy 1846-1873.* Yale University Press. 2016.

11   Power, Samantha. *A Problem from Hell: America and the Age of Genocide.* Basic Books. 2013.

12   Rose, Jacqueline. *The Last Resistance.* Verso. 2013.

13   Freud, Sigmund. *Beyond the*

Pleasure Principle. W.W. Norton and Company. 1990.

14 Nozick, Robert. *Anarchy, State, and Utopia.* Basic Books. 1974.

15 Arendt, Hannah. *Eichmann in Jerusalem: A Report on the Banality of Evil.* Viking. 1968.

16 Goldhagen, Daniel. *Worse Than War: Genocide, Eliminationism, and the Ongoing Assault on Humanity.* Public Affairs. 2009.

17 Malthus, Thomas Robert. *An Essay on the Principles of Population As It Affects the Future Improvements of Society.* J. Johnson in St. Paul's Church Yard.1798.

18 Freedman, David H. *The Truth About Genetically Modified Food.* September 2013. Scientific American.

19 Conway, Gordon. *One Billion Hungry: Can We Feed the World?* Comstock Publishing Associates. 2012.

20 Rotman, David. *Why We Will Need Genetically Modified Foods.* December 2013. MIT Technology Review.

21 Paarlberg, Robert. *Starved for Science: How Biotechnology is Being Kept Out of Africa.* Harvard University Press. 2009.

22 Power, Samantha. *A Problem from Hell: America and the Age of Genocide.* Basic Books. 2002.

23 Voltaire. *Candide, or Optimism.* 1759.

24 Rafizadeh, Majid. *Iran's Forces Outnumber Assad's in Syria.* The Gatestone Institute International Policy Council. November 2016.

25 Daher, Aurélie. *Hezbollah and the Syria Conflict.* The Middle East Institute. November 2015.

26 Erich Fromm. *Escape from Freedom.* Farrar and Reinhart. 1941.

27 Bloxham, Donald. *The Great Game of Genocide: Imperialism, Nationalism, and the Destruction of the Ottoman Armenians.* Oxford University Press. 2007. Olussoga, David and Erichsen, Casper W. *The Kaiser's Holocaust: Germany's Forgotten Genocide and the Colonial Roots of Nazism.* Faber and Faber. 2011.

28 Lemarchand, Réne. *The Dynamics of Violence in Central Africa.* University of Pennsylvania Press. 2007.

29 Prunier, Gerard. *Africa's World War: Congo, the Rwandan Genocide, and the Making of a Continental Catastrophe.* Oxford University Press. 2011. Stearns, Jason. *Dancing in the Glory of Monsters: The Collapse of the Congo and the Great War of Africa.* Public Affairs. 2012.

30 Tim Judah. *The Serbs: History, Myth and the Destruction of Yugoslavia.* Yale University Press. 2010.

31 Paul Collier. *The Bottom Billion: Why the Poorest Countries are Failing and What Can Be Done About It.* Oxford University Press.

2007.

32 Hall, Brian. *The Impossible Country: A Journey Through the last Days of Yugoslavia.* Penguin Books. 1995.

33 Glenny, Misha. *The Fall of Yugoslavia: The Third Balkan War.* Penguin Books. 1996.

34 Marshall McLuhan. *Understanding Media: The Extensions of Man.* McGraw-Hill. 1964.

35 Saleh, Yassin Al-Haj. *Impossible Revolution: Making Sense of the Syr ian Tragedy.* Haymarket Books. 2017.

36 Ghattas, Kim. *Syrian Torture: Will Photos Turn US Opinion.* BBC News. January 2015.

37 Theo Horesh. *Convergence: The Globalization of Mind.* Bauu Institute. 2014.

38 Hasan, Mehdi. *The Palestinians of Yarmouk and the Shameful Silence When Israel is Not to Blame.* The Guardian. April 2015.

39 Chulov, Martin. *Besieged and Terrified, and the Food is About to Run Out for Damascus Refugees.* The Guardian. April 2014.

40 Kerry, John F. *Assad's War of Starvation.* Foreign Policy. October 2013.

41 Hubbard, Ben and Kirkpatrick, David. *Photo Archive is Said to Show Widespread Torture in Syria.* New York Times. January 2014.

42 Slackman, Michael. *Syrian Leader Blames "Conspiracy" for Turmoil.* New York Times. March 2011.

43 Marsh, Katherine and Tisdall, Simon. *Syrian Troops Shoot Dead Protesters in Days of Turmoil.* The Guardian. April 2011.

44 Ghattas, Kim. *US Policy on Syria "Depends on Success in Libya."* The Guardian. May 2011.

45 Saleh, Yassin Al Haj. *Assad's Killing Industry and the Role of Intellectuals.* Al-Jumhuriya. March 2014.

46 Little, Jonathan and Mandell, Charlotte. *Syrian Notebooks: Inside the Homs Uprising.* Verso. 2015.

47 Hokayem, Emile. *Syria's Uprising and the Fracturing of the Levant.* Routledge. 2013.

48 Borri, Francesca. *Syrian Dust: Reporting from the Heart of the War.* Seven Stories Press. 2016.

49 Weiss, Michael and Hassan, Hassan. *ISIS: Inside the Army of Terror.* Regan Arts. 2015.

50 *Ibid*

51 Kassab, Robin Yassin and Al-Shami, Leila. *Burning Country: Syrians in Revolution and War.* Pluto Press. 2016.

52 Van Dam, Nikolaos. *The Struggle for Power in Syria: Politics and Society Under Assad and the Ba'ath Party.* I.B. Tauris. 2011.

53 Saleh, Yassin al-Haj. *Impossible Revolution: Making Sense of the Syrian Tragedy.* Haymarket Books. 2017.

54 Agence France-Presse. *"Era of Propaganda:" Press Freedom in Decline, Says Reporters Without Borders.* The Guardian. April 2016.

55 Carter, Jimmy. *A Five-Nation Plan to End the Syrian Crisis.* New York Times. October 2015.

56 Atzmon, Gilad. *The Wandering Who? A Study of Jewish Identity Politics.* Zero Books. 2011.

57 Lewis, Bernard. *The Jews of Islam.* Princeton University Press. 2014.

58 Gordon, Neve. *Israel's Occupation.* University of California Press. 2008.

59 Carter, Jimmy. *Palestine: Peace Not Apartheid.* Simon and Schuster. 2007.

60 Grossman, David. *The Yellow Wind.* Picador. 2002.Oz, Amos. *In the Land of Israel.* Mariner Books. 1993.

61 Finkelstein, Norman G. *Beyond Chutzpah: On the Misuse of Anti-Semitism and the Abuse of History.* University of California Press. 2008.

62 Morris, Benny. *Righteous Victims: A History of the Zionist-Arab Conflict, 1881-2001.* Vintage. 2001.

63 Morris, Benny. *One State, Two States.* Yale University Press. 2010. Buber, Martin. *A Land of Two Peoples: Martin Buber on Jews and Arabs.* University of Chicago Press. 2005.

64 Pappé, Ilan. *The Ethnic Cleansing of Palestine.* Oneworld Publications. 2007. Khalidi, Rashid. *The Iron Cage: The Story of the Palestinian Struggle for Statehood.* Beacon Press. 2007. Kimmerling, Baruch and Migdal, Joel S. *The Palestinian People: A History.* Harvard University Press. 2003. Morris, Benny. *Righteous Victims: A History of the Zionist-Arab Conflict, 1881-2001.* Vintage. 2001.

65 Sand, Shlomo. *The Invention of the Jewish People.* Verso. 2010.

66 Shavit, Ari. *My Promised Land: The Triumph and Tragedy of Israel.* Spiegel and Grau. 2015. Oz, Amos. *In the Land of Israel.* Mariner Books. 1993.

67 Bregman, Ahron, *Cursed Victory: A History of Israel and the Occupied Territories, 1967 to Present.* Pegasus Books. 2015.

68 Gorenberg, Gershom. *The Unmaking of Israel.* Harper Perennial. 2012.

69 Kimmerling, Baruch. *The Invention and Decline of Israeliness: State, Society, and Military.* University of California Press. 2005.

70 Oz, Amos. *A Tale of Love and Darkness.* Mariner Books. 2005. Grossman, David. *To the End of the Land.* Vintage. 2011. Ben-Ami, Shlomo. *Scars of War, Wounds of Peace: The Israeli-Arab Tragedy.* Oxford University Press. 2007.

71 Hever, Shir. *The Political Economy of Israel's*

Occupation: Repression Beyond Exploitation. Pluto Press. 2010.

72 Shavit, Ari. *My Promised Land: The Triumph and Tragedy of Israel.* Spiegel and Grau. 2015.

73 Barghouti, Mourid. *I Saw Ramallah.* Anchor. 2003. Nusseibeh, Sari. *Once Upon a Country.* Picador. 2008. Shehadeh, Raja. *Strangers in the House: Coming of Age in Occupied Palestine.* Penguin Books. 2003.

74 Chomsky, Noam. *The Fateful Triangle: The United States, Israel, and the Palestinians.* South End Press. 1999.

75 Cook, Jonathan. *Disappearing Palestine: Israel's Experiment's in Human Despair.* Zed Books. 2008.

76 Makdisi, Saree. *Palestine Inside Out: An Everyday Occupation.* W.W. Norton and Company. 2010.

77 Brannon, Susan. *Hebron Settlers.* The Electronic Intifada. July 2002.

78 Herman, Judith. *Trauma and Recovery: The Aftermath of Violence – From Domestic Abuse to Political Terror.* Basic Books. 1997.

79 Van Der Kolk, Bessel. *The Body Keeps the Score: Brain, Mind, and Body in the Healing of Trauma.* Penguin Books. 2015.

80 Levine, Peter A. *Waking the Tiger: Healing Trauma.* North Atlantic Books. 1997.

81 Atzmon, Gilad. *The Wandering Who? A Study of Jewish Identity Politics.* Zero Books. 2011.

82 Berne M.D., Eric. *Games People Play: The Basic Handbook of Transactional Analysis.* Grove Press. 1981. Bowen, Murray. *Family Therapy in Clinical Practice.* Jason Aronson Inc. 1978.

83 Amnesty International. *Israel/ Gaza Conflict. Questions and Answers.* July 2014.

84 Martinez, Michael. *Is Hamas Using Human Shields in Gaza? The Answer is Complicated.* CNN. July 2014.

85 Human Rights Watch. *Soldier's Punishment for Using Boy as "Human Shield" Inadequate.* November 2010.

86 Kimmerling, Baruch and Migdal, Joel S. *The Palestinian People: A History.* Harvard University Press. 2003.

87 Zonszein, Mairav. *Israel killed More Palestinian in 2014 Than in Any Other Year Since 1967.* The Guardian. March 2015.

88 Deutscher, Isaac. *The Non-Jewish Jew and Other Essays.* OUP. 1968.

89 Sartre, Jean Paul. *Anti-Semite and Jew.* Schocken Books. 1948.

90 Arendt, Hannah. *The Origins of Totalitarianism.* Schocken. 1951.

91 Freud, Sigmund. *Moses and Monotheism.* Alfred and Knopf. 1939.

92 Rose, Jacqueline. *The Last*

Resistance. Verso. 2013.

93 Beinhart, Peter. *The Crisis of Zionism.* Picador. 2013.

94 Doyle, Sir Arthur Conan. *The Memoirs of Sherlock Holmes.* The Strand. 1893.

95 Lakoff, George. *Metaphors We Live By.* University of Chicago Press. 2003.

96 Isaac, Jad. *The Role of Groundwater in the Water Conflict and Resolution Between Israelis and Palestinians.* International Symposium on Groundwater Sustainability. Applied Research Institute Jerusalem.

97 Sasson, Talya. *Summary of the Opinion Concerning Unauthorized Outposts.* Israel Ministry of Foreign Affairs. March 2005.

98 Pound, Ezra. *Confucius: The Unwobbling Pivot. The Great Digest. The Analects.* New Directions. 1969.

99 Haas, Amira. *Palestinian Jerusalemites Go Work Abroad and Get Residency Revoked Upon Return.* Haaretz. June 2010.

100 Israeli Committee on House Demolitions. *Comprehensive Briefing on Home Demolitions.* December 2017.

101 McGreal, Chris. *World Court Tells Israel to Tear Down Illegal Wall.* The Guardian. July 10, 2004.

102 Gorenberg, Gershom. *The Unmaking of Israel.* Harper Perennial. 2012.

103 Gordon, Neve. *Israel's Occupation.* University

of California Press. 2008. Makdisi, Saree. *Palestine Inside Out: An Everyday Occupation.* W.W. Norton and Company. 2010.

104 Weizman, Eyal. *Hollow Land: Israel's Architecture of Occupation.* Verso. 2017.

105 Chelala, Cesar. *Destroying Palestinian Olive Trees.* The Globalist. November 2010.

106 Sasson, Talya. *Summary of the Opinion Concerning Unauthorized Outpots.* Israel Ministry of Foreign Affairs. March 2005.

107 *Discriminatory Laws in Israel.* Adalah: The Legal Center for Arab Minority Rights in Israel. 2016.

108 Coursen-Neff, Zama. *Discrimination Against Palestinian Arab Children in the Israeli Education System.* International Law and Politics. Volume 36: 749.

109 New Israel Fund. *Arab Sector: NIF Grantees Fight Discrimination in Arab Education.* December 2005.

110 Shuttlesworth, Kate. *For Arabs in Israel, Curriculum Choice is Politically Charged.* New York Times. January 2014.

111 *Discrimination in land and housing against Palestinian citizens in Israel in 2015.* Adalah: The Legal Center for Arab Minority Rights in Israel. March 2016.

112 Cook, Jonathan. *Disappearing Palestine: Israel's Experiment's in Human*

Despair. Zed Books. 2008. Makdisi, Saree. *Palestine Inside Out: An Everyday Occupation.* W.W. Norton and Company. 2010.

113 Amnesty International. *Discrimination of Palestinians Within Israel.* May 2013.

114 King, Mary Elizabeth. *A Quiet Revolution: The First Palestinian Intifada and Nonviolent Resistance.* Nation Books. 2007.

115 Chenoweth, Erica and Stephan, Maria. *Why Civil Resistance Works: The Strategic Logic of Nonviolent Conflict.* Columbia University Press. 2012.

116 Sharp, Gene and Paulson, Joshua. *Waging Nonviolent Struggle: 20ᵗʰ Century Practice and 21ˢᵗ Century Potential.* Porter Sargent Pub. 2005.

117 Bailey, Sarah Pulliam. *American Evangelicals' Support for Israel is Waning, Reports Say.* Huffington Post. April 2014.

118 Beinhart, Peter. *The Crisis of Zionism.* Picador. 2013.

119 Aslan, Reza. *Zealot: The Life and Times of Jesus of Nazareth.* Random House. 2013.

120 Crossan, John Dominic. *The Historical Jesus: The Life of a Mediterranean Jewish Peasant.* Harper One. 1993.

121 Silberman, Neil Asher and Finkelstein, Israel. *The Bible Unearthed: Archeology's New Vision of Ancient Israel and the Origins of Its Sacred Scriptures.* Touchstone. 2002.

122 Kimmerling, Baruch and Migdal, Joel S. *The Palestinian People: A History.* Harvard University Press. 2003. Morris, Benny. *Righteous Victims: A History of the Zionist-Arab Conflict, 1881-2001.* Vintage. 2001.

123 Levine, Amy-Jill. *The Misunderstood Jew: The Church and the Scandal of the Jewish Jesus.* Harper One. 2007.

124 Borg, Marcus. *The Last Week: What the Gospels Really Teach About Jesus's Final Days in Jerusalem.* Harper One. 2007

125 Sasson, Talya. *Summary of the Opinion Concerning Unauthorized Outposts.* Israel Ministry of Foreign Affairs. March 2005.

126 Chelala, Cesar. *Destruction of Palestinian Olive Trees is a Monstrous Crime.* The Ecologist. November 2015.

127 Ramahi, Sawsen. *Israel is Stealing Palestinian and Arab Water.* Middle East Monitor. May 2014.

128 *Gaza Crisis: Toll of Operations.* BBC. September 2014.

129 Akiva, Eldar. *Netanyahu Has Rejected Two-State Solution.* Al-Monitor. February 2015.

130 Tilley, Virginia. *The One-State Solution: A Breakthrough for Peace in the Israeli-Palestinian Deadlock.* University of Michigan Press. 2010.

131 *Israel: Security Forces Abuse Palestinian Children.* Human Rights Watch. July 2015. *Children in Israeli Military Detention.* United Nations Children's Fund. February 2013.

132 Nusseibeh, Sari. *What is a Palestinian State Worth?* Harvard University Press. 2013.

133 Pinker, Steven. *The Better Angels of Our Nature: Why Violence Declines.* Penguin Books. 2012.

134 Foucault, Michel. *Discipline and Punish: The Birth of the Prison.* Vintage Books. 1995.

135 Horesh, Theo. *Convergence: The Globalization of Mind.* Bauu Institute. 2014.

136 Appiah, Kwame Anthony. *The Honor Code: How Moral Revolutions Happen.* W.W. Norton and Company. 2011.

137 Braley, Alia. *A Nonviolent Grassroots Response to the Islamic State: Strategic Analysis.* Masters Thesis. Harvard University. 2015.

138 Hatzfeld, Jean. *Machete Season: The Killers in Rwanda Speak.* Picador. 2006.

139 Acikyildiz, Birgül. *The Yezidis: The History of a Community, Culture, and Religion.* I.B. Taurus. 2014.

140 Russel, Gerard. *Heirs to Forgotten Kingdoms: Journeys Into the Disappearing Religions of the Middle East.* Basic Books. 2015.

141 Kalyvas, Stathis. *Modern Greece: What Everyone Needs to Know.* Oxford University Press. 2015.

142 Mazower, Mark. *Salonica, City of Ghosts: Muslims and Jews 1430-1950.* Vintage. 2006.

143 Salibi, Kamal. *A House of Many Mansions: The History of Lebanon Reconsidered.* University of California Press. 1990.

144 Young, Michael. *The Ghosts of Martyrs Square: An Eyewitness Account of Lebanon's Life Struggle.* Simon and Schuster. 2014.

145 Hourani, Albert. *A History of the Arab Peoples.* Belknap Press of Harvard University Press. 1991. Hourani, Albert. *Arabic Thought in the Liberal Age 1798-1939.* Cambridge University Press. 1983.

146 Blanford, Nicholas. *Warriors of God: Inside Hezbollah's Thirty-Year Struggle Against Israel.* Random House. 2011. Norton, Augustus Richard. *Hezbollah: A Short History.* Princeton University Press. 2014.

147 Pamuk, Orhan. *Istanbul: Memories and the City.* 2006.

148 Power, Samantha. *A Problem from Hell: America and the Age of Genocide.* Basic Books. 2012.

149 Becker, Ernest. *The Denial of Death.* Free Press. 1997.

150 Holbrook, Richard. *To End a War.* Modern Library. 1999.

151 Power, Samantha. *A Problem from Hell: America and the Age of Genocide.* Basic Books.

2012.

152 Goldhagen, Daniel Jonah. *Worse Than War: Genocide, Eliminationism, and the Ongoing Assault on Humanity.* Public Affairs. 2010.

153 Pinker, Steven. *The Better Angel's of Our Nature: Why Violence Has Declined.* Penguin Books. 2012.

154 Mearsheimer, John J. *The Tragedy of Great Power Politics.* W.W. Norton and Company. 2014.

155 Henry Kissinger. *World Order.* Penguin Books. 2015.

156 Haas, Richard. *World in Disarray: American Foreign Policy and the Crisis of the Old Order.* Penguin Press. 2017. Bremmer, Ian. *Every Nation for Itself: What Happens When No One Leads the World.* Portfolio. 2013.

157 Bengsston, Jesper. *Struggle for Freedom: Aung San Suu Kyi.* Fourth Estate. 2011.

158 Myint-U, Thant. *The Making of Modern Burma.* Cambridge University Press. 2001.

159 Larkin, Emma. *Finding George Orwell in Burma.* Penguin Books. 2006.

160 Anthony Smith. *Nations and Nationalism in a Global Era.* Polity. 1995.

161 Ibrahim, Azeem. *The Rohingyas: Inside Myanmar's Hidden Genocide.* Hurst. 2016.

162 Human Rights Watch. *All You Can Do is Pray: Crimes Against Humanity and Ethnic Cleansing of Rohingya*

Muslims in Burma's Arakan State. April 2013.

163 Myint-U, Thant. *The Making of Modern Burma.* Cambridge University Press. 2001.

164 Victoria, Brian Daizen. *Zen at War.* Rowman and Littlefield Publishers. 2006.

165 Armstrong, Karen. *Fields of Blood: Religion and the History of Violence.* Anchor. 2015. Norenzayan, Ara. *Big Gods: How Religion Transformed Cooperation and Conflict.* Princeton University Press. 2015.

166 *Myanmar: Crimes Against Humanity Terrorize and Drive Rohingya Out.* Amnesty International. October 2017.

167 Human Rights Watch. *Rohingya Crisis.* October 2017.

168 *All You Can Do is Pray: Crimes Against Humanity and Ethnic Cleansing of Rohingya Muslims in Burma's Arakan State.* Human Rights Watch. April 2013.

169 Power, Samantha. *A Problem from Hell: America and the Age of Genocide.* Basic Books. 2012.

170 Browning, Christopher R. *Ordinary Men: Reserve Police Battalion 101 and the Final Solution in Poland.* Harper Perennial. 1998. Goldhagen, Daniel Jonah. *Worse Than War: Genocide, Eliminationism, and the Ongoing Assault on Humanity.* Public Affairs. 2010. Hatzfeld, Jean. *Machete Season: The Killers in Rwanda Speak.*

Picador. 2006.

171 *Malnutrition Amongst Children in Yemen at an All-Time High.* The United Nations Children's Fund. December 2016.

172 Stewart, Phil and Strobel, Warren. *U.S. to Halt Some Arms Sales to Saudis, Citing Civilian Deaths in Yemen Campaign.* Reuters. December 2016.

173 Johnson, Gregory D. *The Last Refuge: Yemen, Al-Qaeda, and America's War in Arabia.* W.W. Norton and Company. 2014.

174 Clark, Victoria. *Yemen: Dancing on the Heads of Snakes.* Yale University Press. 2010. Lackner, Helen. *Why Yemen Matters: A Society in Transition.* Saqi Books. 2014.

175 Lackner, Helen. *Why Yemen Matters: A Society in Transition.* Saqi Books. 2014.

176 Brandt, Marieke. *Tribes and Politics in Yemen: A History of the Houthi Conflict.* Oxford University Press. 2017.

177 Phillip, Sarah. *Yemen and the Politics of Permanent Crisis.* Routledge. 2011.

178 Sen, Amartya. *Development as Freedom.* Anchor. 2000.

179 Dikotter, Frank. *Mao's Great Famine: The History of China's Most Devastating Catastrophe, 1958-1962.* Walker Books. 2011.

180 *Yemen: A Child Under the Age of Five Dies Every 10 Minutes of Preventable Causes – UN Humanitarian Chief.*

United Nations Office for the Coordination of Humanitarian Affairs. January 2017.

181 Lackner, Helen. *Why Yemen Matters: A Society in Transition.* Saqi Books. 2014.

182 De Waal, Thomas. *The Great Catastrophe: Armenians and Turks in the Shadow of Genocide.* Oxford University Press. 2015.

183 Finkelstein, Norman G. *The Holocaust Industry: Reflections on the Exploitation of Jewish Suffering.* Verso. 2015. Segev, Tom. *The Seventh Million: Israelis and the Holocaust.* Picador. 2000.

184 *Africa Review Report on Drought and Desertification.* United Nations Economic and Social Council. Economic Commission for Africa. October 2007.

185 *Nigeria and Boko Haram: The Black Flag in Africa.* The Economist. January 2015.

186 Bird, Christiane. *A Thousand Sighs, A Thousand Revolts: Journeys in Kurdistan.* Ballantine Books. 2004. Lawrence, Quil. *Invisible Nation: How the Kurds Quest for Statehood is Shaping Iraq and the Middle East.* Walker Books. 2008. Mansfield, Stephen. *The Miracle of the Kurds: A Remarkable Story of Hope Reborn in Northern Iraq.* Worthy Publishing. 2014.

187 Power, Samantha. *A Problem from Hell: America and the Age of Genocide.* Basic Books. 2012.

188 Saleh, Yassin Al-Haj. *Impossible Revolution: Making Sense of the Syrian Tragedy.* Haymarket Books. 2017.

189 Freedom House. *Freedom in the World 2017: Freedom Decline Continues Amid Rising Populism and Autocracy.* January 2017.

190 Foreign Policy. *Fragile States Index 2015.* 2015.

191 Kenny, Charles. *Getting Better: Why Global Development is Succeeding – and How We Can Improve the World Even More.* Basic Books. 2012.